ISLINGTON

Librar

mummy
pregnancy cookbook

the yummy mummy
pregnancy cookbook

Hope Ricciotti, MD,
associate professor at
Harvard Medical School

CONSULTANT
Fiona Ford, MSc SRD

London, New York, Melbourne, Munich, Delhi

Project Editors Connie Novis and Norma Macmillan
Project Designer Ruth Hope
Senior Editors Salima Hirani and Jo Godfrey Wood
Senior Art Editor Glenda Fisher
Managing Editor Penny Warren
Managing Art Editor Marianne Markham
Art Director Peter Luff
Category Publisher Corinne Roberts
DTP Designer Sonia Charbonnier
Jacket Designer Candace Lockley
Production Controller Vicky Baldwin
Photographer Sian Irvine

First published in the Great Britain in 2007
by Dorling Kindersley Limited
80 Strand, London WC2R 0RL

A Penguin Company

2 4 6 8 10 9 7 5 3 1

Every effort has been made to ensure that the information contained in this
book is complete and accurate. However, neither the publisher nor the author
is engaged in rendering professional advice or services to the individual reader.
Professional medical advice should be obtained for specific information on
personal health matters. Neither the publisher nor the author accept any legal
responsibility for any personal injury or other damage or loss arising from the
use or misuse of the information and advice in this book.

A CIP catalogue record for this book is available from The British Library

ISBN: 978-1-4053-2035-1

Colour reproduction by Media Development Printing, Great Britain
Printed and bound by Star Standard in Singapore

Discover more at
www.dk.com

contents

foreword

The transition to motherhood is a period of social, psychological, behavioural and biological change in a woman's life and pregnancy is a time when she is more likely to improve her diet and lifestyle and be more receptive to health education messages.

In an ideal world all pregnancies would be planned, so that both mum and dad had an optimum lifestyle, such as not smoking or taking recreational drugs, limiting alcohol and having a healthy diet. But the reality is that in Britain it is estimated that only 50 percent of pregnancies are planned. The stage before pregnancy, when dietary changes should be made, depends on the amount of change required: the more that needs doing, the longer it will take. The most important factor is that the diet should be optimum at conception so, ideally and where possible, women should be encouraged to continue using contraception until they have made the appropriate improvements.

The prevalence of malnutrition (both under- and over-nutrition) among pregnant women increases the risk of low birth weight, prematurity, and excessive prenatal weight gain, with its potential complications. Simply improving people's knowledge about a healthier diet for pregnancy and breastfeeding is not enough. Suitable, healthy foods need to be available, affordable and accessible, and women need the opportunity to learn how to make the right choices and develop their own food budgeting, planning and cooking skills. This book will be an invaluable guide for women who are pregnant, or planning to be, or who have recently had a baby.

Fiona Ford, MSc SRD

introduction

Pregnancy is an exciting time, and one in which many women are highly motivated to do the right thing by eating well to maximize health for themselves and their developing baby.

For many, these changes can spark good habits that last a lifetime. Pregnancy can also be a confusing time, since recommendations are constantly changing, and myths abound. This cookbook puts together the science of nutrition with the art of cooking in simple, understandable ways. A bit of background can clarify a great deal: this is a time when you can enjoy your changing body and the miracle of your developing baby. You can never get enough ideas when it comes to food preparation and this book is a great starting place for both novice and experienced cook.

It's important to get your baby off to a healthy start with the diet you consume during pregnancy. Scientific studies suggests that your diet and weight gain during pregnancy can help prevent serious illnesses later in your baby's life. Keeping your weight within a healthy range can help you feel and look better too. Your health and your baby's health are linked, and this book is good for both of you. Your diet in pregnancy should be exciting and fulfilling. Explore new tastes, since your baby's in utero diet may influence his or her taste buds later in life. Spicy, salty, sweet and sour – they all have a place in a diet for two. Eating for two has a whole new meaning today.

Hope Ricciotti, MD

"This is a time when you can enjoy your changing body and the miracle of your developing baby."

your diet –
your pregnancy

Enjoy your changing body and the miracle of your developing baby. This section helps you plan your pregnancy diet.

why a healthy diet?

Today, we know more about what constitutes a healthy pregnancy diet than we did even 10 years ago. What is clear is that a good, nutritious diet can provide many benefits for you and your baby. And the great news is that it is very simple to achieve the best diet possible. Just keep in mind a few basic principles explained in this book and you can enjoy your pregnancy, and marvel at the extraordinary changes that are taking place in your body.

"What is clear is that a good, nutritious diet can provide many benefits for you and your baby."

Benefits for your baby

The recommendations in this book are based on evidence gathered over the last decade by scientists, nutritionists, and physicians from many different lines of research. Recently, considerable attention has been focused on the diet of a pregnant woman as a perfect opportunity to give the growing foetus the right combination of nutrients and calories that will set it on the road to lifelong good health. Certain vitamins and nutrients can actually prevent birth defects, as well as enhance foetal brain and neural development.

Such common adult disorders as obesity, diabetes, and cardiovascular disease may begin as early as life in the womb, but recent data suggests that prevention can start here, too. In many developed nations today there is an epidemic of obesity and diabetes among women of childbearing age. This has raised concerns over the consequences of foetal overnutrition, which results in high birth weights that can cause health problems later in life. The aim in pregnancy is to eat the right combination of nutrients, while getting enough, but not too many, calories.

building a healthy baby

You can enhance your baby's development by eating a healthy diet while you are pregnant. Consuming certain vitamins and nutrients at this time has been shown to build a better brain and nervous system in your unborn baby.

Building a brain and nervous system

The foetal nervous system is one of the first systems to begin to develop in pregnancy, and it coordinates the development of the other systems. By the end of the first six weeks of pregnancy, the foetus will have established the foundation of its entire nervous system. This system, with its tubular design, is where neural tube defects occur; these are among the commonest of all the possible birth defects. In one in every thousand babies, the neural tube fails to close, leaving the spinal cord partly open to the outside world. This causes a condition known as spina bifida and other related birth defects. However, the incidence of many of these defects can be reduced if you eat foods rich in folate or folic acid (see page 28).

Once the neural tube closes, the brain continues to develop and grow rapidly throughout all three trimesters of pregnancy. You can maximize the development of the foetal brain and nervous system by eating a diet rich in omega-3 fatty acids (see page 27) during this time, and the benefits will last into the baby's childhood as the systems continue to develop.

"The incidence of the most common birth defects can be reduced if you eat foods rich in folate or folic acid."

Heart and blood vessels

Around the fifth week of your pregnancy your baby's heart and blood vessels begin forming. By week seven the heart starts beating. Through the next 33 weeks, as your blood circulates through the placenta, it delivers oxygen and nutrients to fuel your baby's growth, and what you eat supplies the nutrients for this expansion.

The primary fuel supply for your baby is glucose, which comes from the breakdown of dietary carbohydrates into glucose in your bloodstream. Your blood bathes the placenta, and the glucose then crosses the placenta to reach the baby. Supplying your baby with good nutrition early on in the pregnancy enables the placenta, and your baby's blood supply, to develop fully, allowing your baby to achieve his or her maximum genetic growth potential.

Your baby's future health

New research indicates that the risk of cardiovascular disease may be laid down in the diet a baby consumes in the womb. Evidence shows that if you eat a diet high in saturated fat during pregnancy, you may actually increase your baby's risk of developing heart disease, such as atherosclerosis (the build-up of plaque on the inside wall of blood vessels which ultimately blocks them), later in life. On the positive side, you can actively lower the future risk of cardiovascular disease for both you and your baby by eating a heart-healthy diet during your pregnancy. And that's easily done. Simply choose unsaturated and monounsaturated fats such as olive oil, canola (rapeseed) oil, peanut oil, and safflower oil instead of unhealthy saturated and trans fats; limit your intake of beef and full-fat dairy products, which are high in saturated fats; and avoid margarine and processed baked goods, which are high in trans fats.

The third trimester is an important phase of your baby's development because between weeks 28 and 40 your baby will grow by an amazing 350 percent. This is the time during which your baby lays down stores of body fat. Higher glucose levels in your bloodstream after meals are associated with a higher abdominal circumference in your baby. And bigger is not always better when it comes to babies. There are health risks later in life associated with a high birth weight, including obesity, diabetes, and heart disease. But it is easy to keep the glucose levels in your bloodstream at a lower, steadier range by eating unrefined carbohydrates instead of refined starches. (See pages 23 for sources of unrefined carbohydrates.)

BIRTH SIZES

Babies who are big at birth are more likely to have a higher body mass index (BMI) in childhood and adulthood. To this day, the complex way in which the foetus develops in the womb is poorly understood. However, it is known that an elevated level of glucose in the mother's blood is one of the major factors contributing to excessive growth of the foetus. For example, the children of mothers with gestational diabetes have an increased risk of being overweight later in life. Even if you don't have diabetes, the amount of refined carbohydrate you consume affects the levels of glucose in your bloodstream. This in turn has an influence on your baby's growth. Therefore, higher glucose levels, even those in the normal range, can make for a bigger baby. It makes sense to pay attention to what you eat now.

Benefits for you

Pregnancy is a time of dramatic changes in your body – practically every organ and system in your body is altering, and it may seem as if your body no longer even belongs to you. But once you understand what is going on, you can relax because you'll know the changes that are normal and how to take care of yourself. You will gain confidence because you'll know you are maximizing the health and well-being of both of you. You need extra, good-quality fuel for your body's own systems as well as for your baby. Eating well is a simple – and delicious – part of making it work.

Feeling good about yourself and generally keeping a happy, positive outlook will also enhance your physical health and mental well-being. It will prepare you for delivery, ease you through your recovery, and help you regain your pre-pregnancy shape more quickly. Maintaining a healthy lifestyle during your pregnancy will also help you prepare for the rigours of caring for a newborn.

Pregnancy is a great time to create good habits that will be easier to continue as you care for your newborn and grow older together. It is never easy to withstand the sleep deprivation and constant activity in the early months of caring for a

WELL BALANCED, WIDE RANGING
Enjoying a well-balanced, wide-ranging diet following the guidelines in this book will leave you energized and satisfied, and keep you healthy and strong.

newborn, and the best way to get through it is to maintain a good diet throughout your pregnancy and beyond. Poor nutrition during pregnancy can lead to depression and diabetes in the mother, and premature delivery of newborns that are smaller than they should be at birth. It can also lay down future health problems as the child grows up.

It is not always easy to eat well in pregnancy – you are so busy and always seem to be on the go. But you need to keep yourself healthy in order to take good care of your developing baby and your family. Keep the following analogy in mind. On an aeroplane you are asked to put your own oxygen mask on before your child's. Self-care in pregnancy is not selfish; it is smart. You need to take care of yourself first.

Blood pressure

The force that blood exerts on the inside walls of blood vessels is called blood pressure. It is expressed as a ratio, with normal being approximately 120/80 or lower. High blood pressure is defined as 140/90 or higher. The first number is the systolic pressure (the pressure when the heart pushes blood out into the arteries). The second number is the diastolic pressure (the pressure when the heart rests between beats). Your blood pressure decreases in pregnancy, due to the relaxing effect of the hormone progesterone (produced by the placenta) on your blood vessels. This decrease starts in the late first trimester and reaches its lowest point in the second trimester. In the third trimester, most women return to their usual blood pressure.

People with high blood pressure are advised to cut down the amount of salt they consume to a minimum. While your body needs more sodium in pregnancy than at any other time in your life, this doesn't mean you need to increase your dietary salt. Keep processed and fast foods to a minimum, since they tend to be high in salt, and sprinkle the same amount of salt that you normally use on meat and vegetables. Making this a habit that will last beyond your pregnancy will benefit your health; studies show that individuals who have the highest intake of fruits and vegetables, pregnant or not, have the lowest blood pressure.

Your heart and blood in pregnancy

Pregnancy hormones cause your resting heart rate to rise by 10–15 beats, and with every beat of your heart, a larger volume of blood is pumped through your body. By 12 weeks, there will be a marked increase in your heart's output, and it rises further as pregnancy progresses, so that by birth it has increased by about 40 percent. Many women notice that they can hear their heart beating when they lie down.

"Maintaining a healthy lifestyle during your pregnancy will also help you prepare for the rigours of caring for a newborn."

The placenta is a truly amazing organ. It begins to form between 8 and 10 weeks into your pregnancy by growing onto the muscular wall of your uterus. The placenta is the place where oxygen and nutrients are supplied to your baby via your bloodstream, and where carbon dioxide and waste products are returned to your circulation from the baby's for excretion.

The placenta's job does not stop there. It makes a number of hormones in large quantities, including oestrogen and progesterone.

In addition, the placenta serves as the conduit through which substances carried in the bloodstream can be exchanged between mother and foetus, ensuring that your blood and the baby's blood never mix.

Your blood volume expands almost 50 percent by the time you give birth. This means you need to retain salt and water in your body, and additional iron and folate (or folic acid) to fuel the increase in the number of your red blood cells. The extra salt, water, iron, folate, and iron needed to fuel this expansion comes from your diet. (See pages 28–32 for sources of these nutrients.)

Changes in your breasts

The hormones of pregnancy and your increased blood volume cause your breasts to enlarge and become tender. Inside your breasts, a network of milk ducts is developing that will supply milk for your baby. You'll notice your nipples enlarging and darkening. The areolas, the coloured areas surrounding the nipples, become darker in colour, and little bumps appear on them. Your body needs adequate quantities of protein to fuel this development and expansion. (See pages 24–26 for sources of protein.)

Expansion of the uterus

The uterus (or womb), your baby's home during your pregnancy, is a hollow structure with a thick, muscular wall. It is considered the strongest muscle in the human body, and goes from being the size of a peach and weighing about 2oz (60g) to the size of a large watermelon, weighing about 2½lb (1.1kg), by full term. As it is located in the pelvis right behind your bladder, you will find that you urinate frequently as the uterus gets larger, since it takes up some of the space your bladder might normally use. A good amount of protein in your diet is required to fuel the huge expansion of your uterus. (See pages 24–26 for sources of protein.)

The role of calcium

The baby's skeleton begins to form around the end of the first trimester. Toward the end of the second and throughout the third trimester, the amount of calcium the baby takes from your system to develop its skeleton reaches its height. This means calcium is particularly important for your baby in the late second and third trimester. The majority of calcium that your baby needs is transported from your bloodstream through the placenta. Even if you do not have adequate amounts of calcium in your diet and in your bloodstream, whatever calcium you do have will be transported across the placenta, even if it means the baby has high levels of calcium while yours are low. In this way, your baby can meet all of its needs for the formation and mineralization of bones and teeth.

TAKE CARE OF YOURSELF It is not selfish to look after yourself. You need to be fit and well to be able to look after a baby. And the future health and dietary habits of your baby depend on how well you eat during pregnancy.

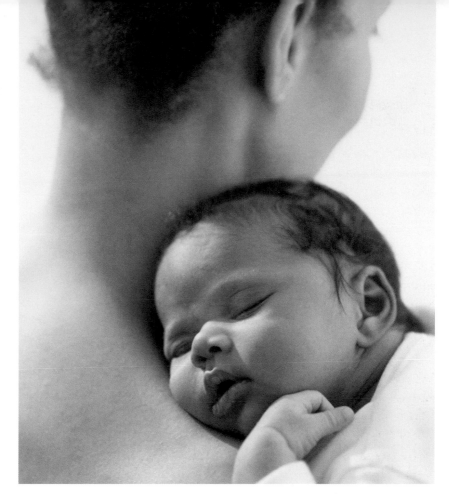

Sharing your calcium

If your blood calcium levels become low due to the amount of calcium your baby is taking up, the calcium in your bones serves as a reservoir to meet your own needs. By constantly replacing lost calcium from the reservoir in your bones, blood calcium levels in your blood will be maintained, despite your baby drawing from them. In the short term, there is some evidence that low dietary calcium can increase the risk of hypertensive disorders in pregnancy; long-term, it can lead to osteoporosis. So for the sake of your health, it is important to get adequate amounts of calcium, especially during pregnancy. (See page 29 for sources of calcium.)

Carrying twins

Twins develop when two eggs are fertilized at the same time (fraternal or non-identical twins) or when a fertilized embryo splits in two (identical twins). Twins can run in families, and older women are also more likely to have them. The changes in your body discussed in this chapter are more dramatic when you are carrying twins.

Once you have become familiar with the principles of healthy eating during pregnancy, it will become second nature to prepare meals and snacks that will bring the greatest possible benefit to you and your baby as well as being delicious and satisfying to eat. There is a lot of information and advice to absorb when you become pregnant, but if you follow the pointers below you can't go wrong with your diet.

In summary...
for a healthy diet

1 **Relax: It's really simple!** Getting the right nutrients during pregnancy to give your baby the best possible start in life is easy to achieve if you eat a well-balanced, wide-ranging diet.

2 **Good for you, too** A healthy diet will keep you strong, positive, and energized, making it easier for you to cope with the big life changes of pregnancy and afterward.

3 **New lifestyle** Pregnancy is a great time to establish new lifestyle habits you can continue in future, as you care for your newborn and for yourself.

4 **Benefits and protection** Your baby will benefit from increased protection from some birth defects and go on to enjoy lifelong benefits if you eat a well-balanced diet.

5 **Brains and nerves** Eating certain vitamins and nutrients during pregnancy has been shown to build a better brain and nervous system in a developing foetus.

6 **Omega-3 fatty acids** Eating foods rich in these enhances your baby's neurological development, helping to build intelligence and promote mental health.

7 **Lower future risks** You can actively lower the future risk of cardiovascular disease in your baby by eating a heart-healthy diet while you are pregnant.

8 **Keep glucose low** High glucose levels in your bloodstream will mean a baby with a high birth weight at risk of obesity, diabetes, and heart disease later in life.

9 **Salt and water** Drink plenty of water and don't hesitate to use the saltshaker on freshly prepared foods while you are pregnant.

10 **Calcium intake** Protect your health by making sure you get enough calcium toward the end of the second trimester and throughout the third.

OMEGA-3 FATTY ACIDS

Enhancing foetal brain development

Studies show that a mother's diet rich in omega-3 fatty acids can enhance a baby's brain and neural development before birth, as well as give protection from neural tube defects.

• Rich sources of omega-3 fatty acids are found in oily fish.

• If you are a vegetarian you need to eat a range of foods to get your sources of omega-3 fatty acids because fish are the only source of all three essential fatty acids (see page 27). Include flax seed, flax seed oil, walnuts, and canola (rapeseed) oil in your diet. Flax seeds must be ground in order for your body to absorb the oil from them.

Italian-style cod recipe (see page 148)

good fuel for
a busy body

"Pregnancy is a
normal state:
we were
making babies
long before we
knew about
nutritional
science."

Pregnancy is a normal state and being pregnant should be looked at in a positive light, not regarded as a disease. After all, we were making healthy babies long before we knew about the science of nutrition in pregnancy. The first chapter (Why a healthy diet?) explained how busy your body is during pregnancy. This chapter will explain which foods are ideal for fuelling all this activity, and will show you just how easy it is to provide yourself with optimum nutrition during your pregnancy.

Eating in pregnancy can be a joy and a pleasure. Enjoy your changed state, indulge your altered palate, and generally celebrate it. At the same time, use being pregnant as an opportunity to re-evaluate your diet and make adjustments that will reward you with health benefits that will last a lifetime.

Sometimes eating right may seem like a time-consuming, labour-intensive challenge. You want to eat the right foods, but your taste buds have changed. You know what a healthy diet is when you are not pregnant, but is this different when you are? And you've heard about some foods that might cause you harm. Armed with a bit of knowledge and some ideas for tempting meals and snacks, you can enjoy your pregnancy while eating delicious foods.

Eating healthily during pregnancy is actually quite simple. Your goal is to provide adequate nutrition for you and your baby, while consuming the appropriate number of calories to achieve the right weight gain.

getting the balance right

Being pregnant does not call for a low-fat, low-carbohydrate diet. Current recommendations for optimum nutrition in pregnancy are to consume 50–60 percent of your calories from carbohydrates, 25–35 percent from fat, and 20 percent from protein.

You have been given a formula to follow, but this does not mean that you must precisely calculate the calories from each component for every meal you consume. If you simply take a big-picture view of your diet using your common sense, achieving this nutrient ratio will become a habit. Once you see a few examples of meals and

"You have been given a formula to follow, but it does not mean that you must precisely calculate the calories from each component at every meal you consume."

menus based on this formula, it will become second nature. It is far from an exact science, and each meal does not need to be composed of a perfect ratio. Remember, a week of eating should approximately fulfil the recommended amounts of each food type. A balanced diet that contains a variety of foods, especially lots of fruits, vegetables, whole grains, heart-healthy proteins, and healthy fats, will provide nearly all the nutrients your body requires (see below).

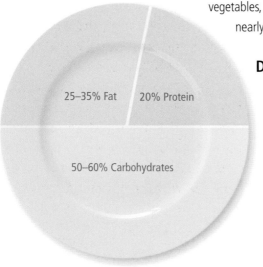

25–35% Fat 20% Protein

50–60% Carbohydrates

Don't count!

While your vitamin and mineral requirements increase during pregnancy, it is not necessary for you to count every vitamin and mineral in your diet. If you follow the advice on healthy eating given in this book you don't need to take supplements, with the exception of folic acid (see page 28).

PREGNANCY DIET FORMULA Keep the ratio of fat, protein, and carbohydrates in the back of your mind and be sure to eat a wide range of foods. This way, you will take in all the nutrients you need, almost without thinking about it.

DAILY CARBOHYDRATE INTAKE

About half of your daily calories should come from carbohydrates, with an emphasis on unrefined sources.

Breakfast Oatmeal with raisins; calcium-fortified orange juice

Lunch Hummus on wholewheat pitta bread; celery sticks; piece of fruit

Dinner Chilli with brown rice

Dessert Fruit with whipped cream

carbohydrates

You need carbohydrates as your "basic" fuel, and that's where you should consume about 50–60 percent of your calories. This translates into about six servings of carbohydrates every day from any food made from wheat, rice, oats, cornmeal, or another cereal grain. A serving can be a slice of bread, half a bagel, or 150g (5¼oz) of a cereal grain.

Grains are divided into two subgroups, refined and unrefined. Unrefined grains contain the entire grain kernel – the bran, germ, and endosperm. You should try to obtain at least half, if not all, of your carbohydrate intake from unrefined grains.

Refined or unrefined?

What is the difference between a refined and an unrefined grain? From a miller's standpoint, refined starches and sugars have undergone a process that removes the bran and germ to give grains a finer texture. However, this process also removes dietary fibre and nutrients, so from a health standpoint, unrefined grains are better for you and your baby. They break down more slowly in your body, and release glucose in a steady manner, avoiding the spikes of glucose in your bloodstream that follow when you eat refined grains. Studies suggest that this is a healthier way to eat.

Avoiding peaks and valleys

Both your and your baby's body prefer a steady release of glucose, avoiding the peaks and valleys caused by the intake of refined starches and sugars. When you eat refined carbohydrates, such as white rice, white bread, and sweets, or drink sweet fizzy drinks, they enter your bloodstream quite rapidly, resulting in a large spike in glucose levels. It is thought these spikes may result in larger babies at birth, who are at risk of being overweight or obese as they grow up. So stick to unrefined grains as the basis for your pregnancy diet, and save white bread and white rice for only once in a while. You can still eat sweet things, but keep portions small and save them for treats. While refined grains are not forbidden, you should still try to get the majority of grains in your diet from unrefined sources (see page 37).

DAILY NON-VEGETARIAN PROTEIN INTAKE

Getting about 60g (2oz) of protein per day is easy if you include some protein in all meals. Look at the following example:

Breakfast Two hard-boiled omega-3-enriched eggs; wholewheat toast; orange juice

Lunch Spicy lentil and cauliflower soup (see recipe, page 124); green salad with olive oil and balsamic vinegar dressing; slice of crusty bread

Dinner Simply quick pan-fried steak (see recipe, page 155); Roasted asparagus with pine nuts and blue cheese (see recipe, page 135)

Dessert Walnut and chocolate chip cookies (see recipe, page 174)

protein power

Protein is required to fuel the physical growth and cellular development of your baby, placenta, and amniotic tissues, as well as your blood expansion, uterine growth, and breast development. Twenty percent of your daily calories should come from protein, and most women have no problem meeting their protein requirements.

You need 60g (2oz) of protein daily in pregnancy, which translates into about three daily servings. If all of your protein sources are vegetarian, aim for four servings daily. Protein sources include meat, poultry, fish, tofu, beans, milk, cheese, yogurt, eggs, nuts, and seeds. If you eat cereal with milk for breakfast, a peanut butter sandwich for lunch, and a piece of meat or fish with beans for dinner, it adds up to about 70g (2½oz) of protein. So, if you have protein at all three meals, you'll get enough. Most sources of protein contain some fat, so aim to eat sources of protein that are low in saturated fat, such as fish, nuts, and seeds, which contain healthy oils. Bear in mind that you can consume up to 350g (12oz) of fish per week in pregnancy (see page 35), as long as you avoid fish that are high in mercury.

Eliminating unhealthy fats is easy

You can reduce your intake of unhealthy fat from protein sources by removing the skin from poultry. When you are choosing dairy protein, you can keep the saturated fat content to a minimum by using low-fat cheese and products made from skimmed milk whenever possible. You do not need to eliminate beef and pork altogether, but limit them to once a week as part of a heart-healthy diet and remember that certain cuts are lower in saturated fat than others. Trim away all of the visible fat from

meats before cooking, and grill, roast, or poach them instead of frying. A portion of 85g (3oz) of meat (approximately the size of a deck of cards) makes the ideal serving size. Leaner choices of beef that are still delicious include tenderloin, sirloin, flank steak, first-cut brisket, and 90 percent lean hamburger. Well-trimmed pork tenderloin can also be a good choice because the fat content is lower than that of white-meat chicken. The confusion with pork is that in addition to lean cuts, there are also fatty cuts, such as spare ribs, bacon, and ham, which are high in saturated fats. The leanest and most tender cuts come from the loin, and are best cooked by sautéeing or grilling them.

Nutritional nuts

Nuts are a great source of protein, folic acid, and heart-healthy oils, but serious allergies to nuts and nut products and some seeds affect about 1–2 percent of people in the UK. Your baby may be at higher risk of developing a nut allergy if you, your baby's father, or your brothers and sisters have certain allergic conditions such as hayfever, asthma, and/or eczema. There is a degree of controversy about the consumption of nuts during pregnancy, but if your baby is in this higher-risk group you may wish to be on the safe side and avoid eating peanuts and peanut products when you are pregnant and breastfeeding. Otherwise, peanuts are a great source of heart-healthy protein, oils, and folic acid, so those without any allergies in the family should indulge.

Protein and the vegetarian

All proteins are made up of amino acids, but they are not all alike. Amino acids are the building blocks of protein, and there are 23 of them, divided into two types – essential and non-essential. All 23 amino acids are needed for your and your baby's health, but the word "essential" refers to the fact that 8 of them must be provided ready to absorb from your diet. Your body can manufacture the other 15,

Here is how a vegetarian can get enough protein:

Breakfast Nutty granola (see recipe, page 104) in vanilla yogurt, with fruit

Lunch Wholewheat rollups with tangy white beans and vegetables (see recipe, page 114); skimmed milk

Snack Mixed nuts

Dinner Spaghetti with asparagus and toasted walnuts (contains cheese) (see recipe, page 144)

Dessert Walnut and chocolate chip cookie (see recipe, page 174) with skimmed milk

non-essential, amino acids itself, by converting and remodelling them from the foods you eat. Think of the 8 essential amino acids like the primary colours red, yellow, and blue. You can make any colour from these 3, but you can't make the primaries from any other colours. Analogous to this, the 15 non-essential amino acids can all be made from the 8 essential amino acids, for a total of 23 amino acids, just as all the colours of the rainbow can be made from the 3 primary colours. The classification system simply tells you whether or not your body is capable of manufacturing a particular amino acid, but you need to consume a certain amount of all of them for good health.

Complete and incomplete proteins

A complete protein contains all the 23 amino acids that are required by your body, but incomplete proteins may be combined in your diet to fully supply your nutritional needs. Your body stores amino acids from the protein that you eat, so you do not need to obtain all 23 amino acids in one meal. Animal sources of protein, such as beef, chicken, fish, and dairy products, tend to be complete. Other protein sources lack one or more amino acids that your body can't manufacture itself. These incomplete proteins usually come from beans, seeds, vegetables, grains, and nuts. However, they can be combined to add up to a complete protein that contains all the necessary amino acids.

A vegetarian diet is safe in pregnancy, but you need to pay attention to getting adequate amounts of protein, since vegetarian sources tend to be slightly lower than animal proteins. You need to vary the protein sources so that you are certain to get all the essential amino acids. Vegetarians can make up for incomplete proteins by eating a variety. That way, if some amino acids are missing in one protein source, you'll be more likely to get them from another source. The various amino acids you need can be consumed over several meals. It is not necessary for each meal to contain complementing proteins. You can consume a variety of protein sources over the course of the day to collect all 23 essential amino acids.

STIR-FRIED VEGETABLES This vegetarian dish of Stir-fried pak choy and sweet peppers with roasted tofu (see page 108 for recipe) will give you a wide range of vitamins and essential nutrients.

The total amount of fat you can consume in healthy quantities on a daily basis if all your fat comes from oils amounts to about 3 tablespoons. The following is an example of a day of healthy eating with the majority of fat coming from unsaturated sources, adding up to about 30 percent of your total daily calories. (Sources of fat are given in italics.)

Breakfast A slice of wholewheat toast lightly spread with *butter*; cereal with skimmed milk

Lunch A generous-sized salad with a dressing based on *olive oil* and a few ounces of reduced-fat *Cheddar cheese* on your salad and some crusty wholegrain bread

Dinner *Salmon* with a side of greens and a baked potato drizzled with *olive oil*

Dessert A single scoop of low-fat *frozen yogurt*

the lowdown on fats

Healthy fats fuel your body and serve as the basis for fat-soluble vitamins and hormones, and should make up 25–35 percent of your diet. Some fats are bad for you, while others are good. Saturated fats, found in meat and dairy products, can contribute to high cholesterol, heart disease, an increased risk of some cancers, and obesity.

Trans fats, found in margarine, fast food, and processed baked goods, are also unhealthy. Focus on keeping the majority of fat in your diet from healthy fats rather than trying to achieve a low-fat diet. What really matters is the type of fat you eat and the key is to substitute good fats for bad fats.

Omega-3 fatty acids

Studies show that a maternal diet rich in omega-3 fatty acids can enhance a baby's brain and neural development throughout pregnancy and while you are breastfeeding. Omega-3 fatty acids are found in rich amounts in oily fish, the only source of all three essential omega-3 fatty acids. They are called "essential" because they cannot be made in your body, but need to be supplied by your diet. There are three principal omega-3 fatty acids – alpha-linolenic acid (ALA), eicosapentaenoic acid (EPA), and docosahexaenoic acid (DHA). The problem is that many of the fish that are rich in these fatty acids are also high in mercury, which can be harmful to the baby's developing nervous system. There are two fish – salmon and anchovies – that are rich in omega-3 fatty acids yet not high in mercury. Wild salmon is particularly rich, but farm-raised salmon is also a good choice. Wild salmon is a pregnancy superfood, because it is very high in omega-3 fatty acids, as well as being a heart-healthy protein source, not to mention delicious. Anchovies are not everyone's favourite, but using them as an ingredient may change your mind.

There are vegetarian sources of omega-3 fatty acids. These include flax seed, flax seed oil, walnuts, and canola (rapeseed) oil. Eggs enriched with omega-3 fatty acids (produced by hens fed flax seed) are also available, and they too are a pregnancy superfood. These foods are all good sources of the essential omega-3 ALA. Note that flax seed must be ground in order for your body to absorb it, or it will pass through you undigested.

DAILY IRON
INTAKE

Here is a daily diet that
contains 14.8mg of iron
with nutrients to increase
its absorption. (Sources of
iron are given in italics.)
Breakfast *Wholegrain-
enriched cereal* with
chopped dates
Lunch *Split pea soup* with
crackers and cheese chunks
Afternoon snack Handful
of *almonds* and a glass of
orange juice
Dinner *Steak* with a side
of *spinach*, sweet potato
chips and tomato slices

**DAILY FOLATE
INTAKE**

Here is a daily diet that
supplies 300mcg of folate.
(Sources of folate are given
in italics.)
Breakfast *Cereal* with
sliced *strawberries*
Lunch *Avocado* and
cheese in a wholewheat
sandwich with lettuce and
tomato
Afternoon snack
Sunflower seeds
Dinner *Chicken* served
with *Swiss chard* and
oven chips

other essential nutrients

There are a number of other essential nutrients you need during
pregnancy to support the changes taking place in your body and to
enhance your baby's development. All are easy to obtain through diet.

Iron

The volume of blood in your body will increase by about 50 percent by the time you
give birth, so you need more iron in your diet to support this increase. Folate, along
with iron, supports the expansion of blood volume that occurs during pregnancy (see
Folate below). The amount of iron you need while pregnant is 14.8mg per day. Many
foods contain iron, and eating a wide range of foods can help most people meet their
needs for this nutrient. Being deficient in iron can lead to iron-deficiency anaemia, a
condition that can leave you feeling tired and run down. Your baby will get enough
iron from you for building its own red blood cells and other needs, even if you do not
have adequate iron intake and stores, but it will be at your expense. The majority of
iron is transferred to the baby in the third trimester, so pay particular attention to
the iron in your diet at that point.

Iron in foods takes two forms: haem iron, found in meat, poultry, and fish, and
non-haem iron, found in plant foods. Haem is an iron-carrying substance found in
human beings and animals, and is produced in the red blood cells. Your body can
absorb haem iron more easily than non-haem iron. Absorption of the latter is
enhanced by foods rich in vitamin C, and inhibited by phytates (in cereals and pulses),
fibre, tannins (in tea and coffee), and calcium. For example, drinking orange juice
while you eat a meal boosts your absorption of the iron in your meal, while taking
tea and coffee with that same meal will inhibit the amount of iron you absorb.

Folate and folic acid

Folate is a B vitamin that is produced in synthetic form as folic acid. There is now
conclusive evidence that increasing intakes of folate through supplements of folic
acid before conception and during the first 12 weeks of pregnancy prevents the
majority of neural tube defects, for example spina bifida, in babies. It is therefore
recommended that all women of child-bearing age, and especially those who are
planning a pregnancy or are in the early stages of pregnancy, take a daily supplement
of 400mcg of folic acid as it is difficult to achieve this amount of additional folate

Here is a daily diet that contains 800mg of calcium. (Sources of calcium are given in italics.)

Breakfast Non-fat *yogurt* with mixed fruit sprinkled with *almonds*. *Calcium-fortified orange juice*

Lunch Toasted *Cheddar cheese* and tomato sandwich on wholewheat bread

Afternoon snack *Sunflower seeds* and glass of *skimmed milk*

Dinner *Tofu* and mixed vegetable stir-fry

YOGURT, FRESH BERRIES, AND NUTS Create your own nutrient-packed treat using fresh fruits.

by means of diet alone. So important is the role of increased folate pre-conception and in the first stages of pregnancy that in many countries grain products are fortified with folic acid as a public health measure.

Combine the folic acid supplement with a folate-rich diet to supply 300mcg, making a total of 700mcg per day. There are abundant good sources of folate, which include most fruits and vegetables, chicken, fish, and fortified grains. Eat them in delicious combinations, and know that both you and your baby are benefiting. Many studies show that folate or folic acid has numerous health benefits outside of pregnancy, among them reducing the risk of heart disease and cancer.

Calcium

Calcium will build your baby's bones and protect your own during pregnancy. The recommended daily allowance of calcium in pregnancy is 800mg. Calcium is found in rich amounts in dairy products. It is important to realize that you get just as much from skimmed and low-fat dairy products as you do from whole-milk dairy products because the calcium is not contained in the fat portion of the milk. Removing the fat does not remove any of the calcium; in fact, removing the fat actually concentrates the calcium a bit more. And since the fat in dairy is saturated fat (an unhealthy fat), you should try to emphasize non-fat or low-fat dairy products in your diet. Choose skimmed milk, non-fat yogurt, and low-fat cheese for the majority of your dairy products.

In order to absorb calcium from food, you also need to take in adequate vitamin D (400 IUs). Although vitamin D is made in the skin by the action of sunlight, in many parts of the world there is not enough exposure for this to be an adequate source. In addition, many of us work indoors for much of the day. Sunscreen filters also reduce much of the vitamin D. However, it can also be obtained from fortified cereal and from dairy foods, in particular milk.

Vegetarian sources of calcium These include dark green, leafy vegetables, as pwell as tofu, which is processed with calcium. Broccoli and romaine lettuce are good sources, so indulge in a nice salad made with the latter, and add some shavings of Parmesan cheese, for a calcium punch. Soya milk is fairly low in calcium compared to cow's milk (about 80mg in an average glass compared to 300mg). Phytic acid, found in Swiss chard, spinach, tea, and most grains, seeds, and beans, reduces your body's ability to absorb calcium, so if you want to increase your calcium intake, these should be avoided or ingested in limited quantities.

DAILY ZINC INTAKE

Here is a daily diet containing 15mg of zinc. (Sources of zinc are given in italics.)

Breakfast *Cereal* with *raisins*

Lunch *Peanut butter* and sliced banana on *wholewheat bread*

Afternoon snack *Pumpkin seeds* and an orange

Dinner *Pork chops*, apple sauce, potatoes

Zinc

Zinc is an essential nutrient for growth and development in pregnancy, and you need 50 percent more zinc when you are pregnant, which amounts to 15mg a day. Deficiencies in zinc have been linked with birth defects, restricted foetal growth, and premature delivery, and even mild zinc deficiency has been related to complications of labour and delivery. Foods of animal origin, including meat and seafood, contain more zinc than their plant-based counterparts, and the zinc is better absorbed and used by the body. Although legumes, nuts, and whole grains are good sources of zinc, the absorption of the zinc in a usable form by your body is lower than it is for animal products because of the phytic acid content (see Calcium, page 29). Vegetarians can overcome this by eating larger quantities of these foods.

Fruits and vegetables

Fruits and vegetables are vital for a healthy diet, and variety is as important as quantity. No single fruit or vegetable provides all of the nutrients you and your baby need to be healthy. The key lies in the range of different fruits and vegetables that you eat. Eating a variety will enable you to obtain, in the amounts you need, other vital nutrients such as vitamins A, C, K, and E, B vitamins (including folate and niacin), phosphorus, iron, calcium, and zinc, as well as fibre.

PRAWNS ARE A GOOD SOURCE OF ZINC However, if you have a shellfish allergy it is essential to use other sources of zinc and avoid any foods to which you are allergic, no matter how high in nutrients they are.

Aim for a minimum of five servings of fruits and vegetables daily, but more is better. There really is no limit to the amount of vegetables you can consume in your diet, and studies show that nine servings of fruits and vegetables a day is ideal. Fruit can be eaten fresh or dried. Vegetables may be eaten cooked, raw, or prepared from frozen. Another good choice is 100 percent vegetable juice. Don't go overboard on 100 percent fruit juice, though, because it is high in sugar and calories. You are much better off nutritionally with the whole fruit rather than just the juice, since much of the fibre and nutrients can be lost in the juicing process, so limit fruit juice to about one serving a day.

Try a wider variety of vegetables, making sure you include dark green, leafy vegetables as well as yellow, orange, and red vegetables, and don't forget cooked tomatoes. Go for a rainbow of colours and you'll benefit nutritionally and enjoy a variety of flavours. Eat as many different fruits, including citrus fruits, as possible, and remember that fibre is great for relieving constipation.

Fibre

Dietary fibre, the indigestible portion of plant foods, is important for good health at all times. It is the best natural way to keep your bowels moving. Filling up on fibre can help you feel full for longer, and can therefore help you keep within the recommended weight gain in pregnancy. Fibre has been linked to managing diabetes, cutting cholesterol, and limiting heart disease. You should consume between 1 and 1¼oz (25 and 35g) of fibre a day. While that might not sound like a lot, most individuals only get about ½oz (15g), pregnant or not, and many people consume much less. Fibre can be found in most fruits and vegetables.

Water

Staying hydrated allows for the expansion of the volume of your blood which normally takes place during pregnancy. Because much of the fluid you take in leaks into your tissues and does not stay in your bloodstream, you often need quite a lot of water in order to stay hydrated. While there is no exact amount that hydrates everyone, approximately six to eight 8fl oz (250ml) glasses of water or other fluid per day is average. You can tell whether or not you are hydrated by the colour of your urine. If it is bright yellow, you are dehydrated. If it is light yellow to clear, you are well hydrated. Staying hydrated will prevent preterm labour, headaches, kidney stones, constipation, and haemorrhoids, as well as minimize the common feelings of light-headedness and dizziness in pregnancy.

other considerations

During pregnancy it's natural to be extra concerned about whether your diet is giving the best possible start to your baby, especially if you follow a particular dietary regime. General health guidance such as the amount of salt you should have in your food will also become more important to you.

Dietary guidelines for vegans

Ensure you eat a hearty portion of protein at each meal, and have a daily protein snack in the afternoon or evening. Drinking soya milk is a good way to add some extra protein. Try to consume beans such as chickpeas, and black, white, or red kidney beans about once a day. Try different kinds of lentils as well, and use brown rice and wholewheat breads. Snack regularly on a variety of nuts and seeds.

There are no natural sources of vitamin B12 available for a vegan diet. Vegans should eat foods fortified with vitamin B12, such as yeast extracts, vegetable stock, veggie burgers, textured vegetable protein, soya milk, vegetable and sunflower margarines, and breakfast cereals.

To ensure adequate zinc, keep wheatgerm handy and sprinkle it on zinc-fortified cereal. Snack on nuts and seeds, especially pumpkin seeds, since they are particularly rich in zinc. Luckily, many of the protein sources you will naturally be consuming as a vegan, such as beans, legumes, tofu, and miso, are good sources of zinc.

Salt consumption

Salt regulates fluid balance in cells and blood. During pregnancy and breastfeeding, more salt is needed than at any other time of life, but sufficient can be obtained from a normal healthy diet. During pregnancy, your blood volume expands by 50 percent, and this increase requires salt. Years ago, pregnant women were told to restrict salt to prevent high blood pressure related to pregnancy, but recent scientific evidence has not supported this. In addition, restricting the amount of salt you consume will not decrease the normal swelling during pregnancy that all women experience to varying degrees. Most of the salt in your diet comes from processed foods and fast food, so your best bet is to salt your food to taste at home to enhance the flavours of lean meats and vegetables and limit your intake of processed and fast foods.

VEGETABLE SOUP A homemade vegetable soup provides a filling and delicious lunch or starter to an evening meal. For convenience, make a large quantity and put some away in the freezer.

Plan your meals

Now's a great time to launch your family into a lifetime of healthy eating. Sit down on a Saturday and plan an entire week of breakfasts, lunches, dinners, and snacks. Once all of the ingredients have been listed, cross off the items that you already have in the cupboard.

Shop once a week

Multiple stops at the supermarket are inefficient and lead to a grocery bill that is unnecessarily high. Many of the recipes in this book emphasize simple preparations and fresh ingredients that highlight the natural flavours and textures of the food you are cooking.

Stock your kitchen

In a well-stocked kitchen, nourishing meals are as near as the cupboard. You'll be able to come home from work and prepare healthy meals in a short space of time.

healthy eating made easy

There is just no substitute for home cooking when it comes to staying healthy and eating well, which is particularly important when you are pregnant. The initial step, and arguably the most important, in cooking delicious and healthful meals at home is meticulous planning.

Cooking at home

Home cooking can be very easy, and you can complete a meal in about the same amount of time it takes to order and pick up a takeout – and it is much cheaper. This book will show you how to get organized and get cooking for a lifetime. Plan ahead and stock a good pregnancy pantry. The solution lies in advance planning, organization, and being aware of your changing nutritional needs. Home cooking is the only way to stay healthy for life. Eating is a pleasurable and fulfilling experience for the whole family, and home cooking doesn't have to take all day.

When you cook at home, you are setting a positive example for your children, eating fabulous foods, and saving money. Many scientific studies support the notion that families that eat together have better mental health, eat more fruits and vegetables, and have children who perform better at school. Starting these habits when your children are babies will put you on the right road as a family for life. With just a bit of effort, you can learn about ingredients and basic cooking techniques, and acquire lifelong kitchen skills.

The tips shown left simplify home cooking. They take away the daily headache of deciding what to eat and make the organizing of ingredients simple, leaving you to enjoy cooking quick meals and tossing together healthy, delicious snacks and lunchboxes with ease.

Organic food

Consuming organic foods is one way to eat in a more healthy fashion. Organic food is produced without using pesticides or bioengineering. Organic meat, poultry, eggs, and dairy products come from animals that are not given antibiotics or growth hormones. Choosing organic foods also benefits the environment, since organic farming promotes the use of renewable resources, as well as soil and water conservation. This helps to safeguard the health of the planet for future generations.

> "Eating is a pleasurable and fulfilling experience for the whole family, and home cooking doesn't have to take the whole day."

An increasing number of supermarkets now carry a range of fresh organic produce, due to growing demand. Organic foods and other produce have the fewest chemical residues and additives, but do cost more than regular produce. Although they often taste much better, organic fruit and vegetables may not appear to be as free of blemishes as those you are used to seeing in supermarkets, but don't let a few brown spots deter you from buying them.

This advice is not intended to make you nervous about eating supermarket produce, and it is important to remember that not all meats are pumped full of antibiotics and not all fruits and vegetables are coated with harmful amounts of pesticides. Most additives are safe during pregnancy – after all, most women don't change their diets much during pregnancy and still have perfectly healthy babies. The most important step in eating a healthy diet is to cook from whole foods and fresh fruits and vegetables. Eating organic is a second step that adds to a healthy foundation of good eating.

Foods to leave out

There are some food precautions related to diet that you need to be aware of in pregnancy. When you are armed with the knowledge of foods to include and omit, both you and your baby will thrive. In general, common sense will see you through your pregnancy (see box).

FOOD PRECAUTIONS

• Listeria is a bacteria to which pregnant women are especially susceptible. Avoid lunchmeats, hot dogs, or prepared deli foods (including cook-chill foods) unless you reheat them thoroughly. Do not eat soft cheeses, unless they are made with pasteurized milk, pâté, or raw seafood.

• An infection caused by a parasite, toxoplasmosis can cause severe problems, especially in the first trimester. Cook all beef, pork, and lamb until medium-well done.

• Salmonella bacteria can cause high fever, vomiting, diarrhoea, and dehydration in the mother, though they do not directly harm the baby. Avoid raw eggs, keep prepared foods chilled, and do not eat unpasteurized dairy products.

• Nearly all fish contain harmless amounts of mercury, but it accumulates in large predator fish. Avoid swordfish, shark, and marlin, as well as freshwater fish. To stay within safe limits, have no more than two portions of oily fish such as tuna, mackerel, sardines and trout per week.

• Do not have more than 300mg of caffeine (4 cups instant coffee, 3 cups brewed coffee, or 6 cups of tea) a day; high levels can result in babies of a low birth weight or even miscarriage. Caffeine is also present in other drinks such as cola and in chocolate.

Now you're pregnant, take this opportunity to check your diet and eat really well. What you eat in pregnancy will give you and your growing baby all the nutrition needed to keep you both strong and healthy, plus your baby gets an excellent start in life. Plan your meals and snacks and cook some really delicious meals for yourself and your family. Use the list below to remind you of the most important points discussed in this chapter.

In summary...
good fuel

1 **Pregnancy is a perfectly normal state** We were making healthy babies long before we knew about nutritional science. Being pregnant isn't being ill.

2 **Balance your intake** Consume 50–60 percent of your calories from carbohydrates, 25–35 percent from fat, and 20 percent from protein.

3 **Don't count!** A diet with a wide variety of healthy foods will supply you and your baby with all the nutrients that you need.

4 **Go unrefined** Stick with unrefined grains as the basis of your diet and save white bread, white pasta, and white rice for occasional treats.

5 **Don't avoid fats** What matters is the type of fat you eat. Focus on getting the majority of fat in your diet from healthy fats, rather than trying to achieve a low-fat diet.

6 **Folate or folic acid** Bump up your intake of folate and folic acid while you are trying to conceive and in the first twelve weeks of your pregnancy.

7 **Fill up on fibre** You will feel fuller longer and will avoid constipation and excessive weight gain if you eat lots of fruits and vegetables, which are rich in fibre.

8 **Home cooking** Prepare your own meals because it's healthier and cheaper too! Cooking from home also reduces the risk of exposure to listeria bacteria.

9 **Whole food health** To get the best nutrients, cook with whole foods and fresh fruits and vegetables. If you want, go one step further and buy organic.

10 **Caffeine and alcohol** You can have small daily amounts of caffeine, and a maximum of 1 or 2 units of alcohol, once or twice a week.

UNREFINED AND REFINED GRAINS

You should try to make a point of eating at least six servings a day of unrefined grains and save refined grains for treats only.

Unrefined grains:

Wholewheat bread
Wholewheat cereals
Wholewheat crackers
Wholewheat pasta
Wholewheat tortillas
Bulghur (cracked wheat)
Kasha
Quinoa
Wholegrain cold cereals
Wholegrain couscous

Wholegrain waffles
Oatmeal
Whole cornmeal
Brown rice

Grains, 1 serving:
½ wholewheat bagel
Slice wholewheat bread
45g (1½oz) cereal
85g (3oz) cooked bulghur
5 wholegrain crackers

½ wholewheat muffin
125g (4½oz) porridge
4in (10cm) pancake
75g (2½oz) cooked pasta
85g (3oz) rice
6in (15cm) tortilla

Refined grains:
White flour
White bread
White rice

how much weight?

Neither you nor the baby benefit if you go above the upper limit of recommended weight gain. Putting on too much weight can make you uncomfortable and leave you with a large amount of extra weight to lose later. But never skip meals in pregnancy. Your baby is constantly drawing glucose off your bloodstream, and if you don't replenish your energy supply regularly you'll find yourself low on energy and even light-headed. Eat three meals a day, and have snacks on hand as well.

"Everyone gains weight in a slightly different fashion in pregnancy, so just keep your target weight in mind."

Calories and weight goals

You need 200 more calories a day during your pregnancy, depending on your physical activity. The recommended weight gain is 11.3–15.8kg (25–35lb) for women of normal weight. "Normal weight" means that your body mass index is between 20 and 25. If you are overweight, you can safely limit your weight gain to 6.8kg (15lb), and if you are underweight or pregnant with twins, you should gain up to 18kg (40lb).

A total weight gain of 11.3–15.8kg (25–35lb) (translates into about 1.3–2.7kg (3–6lb) of weight gain in the first trimester, and 2.7–5.4kg (6–12lb) weight gain in both second and third. This averages out to 225–450g (½–1lb) per week over the 40 weeks of pregnancy.

Don't feel you have to focus on your week-to-week gain. Everyone gains weight in a slightly different fashion, so just keep your target weight in mind. These guidelines help to ensure you gain enough weight to give you and your baby adequate nutrition, without putting on too much. Remember, the baby does not gain further benefits if you exceed the guideline weights, and studies show you are more likely to be able to return to your pre-pregnancy weight if you stay within the guidelines. If you exceed the upper limit, the weight you retain goes up exponentially. Therefore, one of the best ways to prevent excess weight later in life is to eat moderately, stay active, and not gain too much weight in pregnancy.

weight gain

Staying at the optimum weight during pregnancy is a balancing act. Gaining too much weight or putting on too little is not good for you, nor for your developing baby. You may also feel very hungry during pregnancy and at other times struggle with nausea. Yet at the same time, you must not skip meals or neglect to make sure you have a wide-ranging nutritional intake. The guidelines here will help to ensure that you and your baby receive adequate nutrition, without your putting on too much weight.

Components of pregnancy weight gain

About 900g–1.3kg (2–3lb) are from fluid retention, 1.3–1.8kg (3–4lb) from increased blood volume, 450–900g (1–2lb) from breast enlargement, 900g–1.3kg (2–3lb) from enlargement of the uterus, and 900g–1.3kg (2–3lb) from amniotic fluid. At full term, the baby may weigh 2.7–4kg (6–8lb) and the placenta 450–900g (1–2lb). This leaves an actual increase of only about 1.8–2.7kg (4–6lb) in maternal fat.

RECOMMENDED WEIGHT GAIN IN PREGNANCY

If your body weight before pregnancy was normal (BMI 20–25) and you gain the recommended 11.3–15.8kg (25–35lb) during your pregnancy, keep in mind that very little of this weight gain is actually in the form of fat. It is what is known as lean body gain, and you should not regard it as either unhealthy or unsightly.

Studies show that women who eat according to the demands of their appetite during pregnancy, and stay physically active, gain an average of 13kg (28lb), which is well within the guidelines for proper weight gain for women of normal weight. Your body will guide you in the right direction, so it's wise to pay attention to it.

There are many components in pregnancy that contribute to your overall weight gain. The heaviest component, is, of course, the baby itself, but the amniotic fluid, fluid retention in your body, and uterine enlargement are the next heaviest, with breast enlargement and the placenta being the lightest. All the weight gain ranges listed above represent the baby at full term.

CHOCOLATE CRAVING Rather than indulging your chocolate cravings by eating an entire bar of chocolate on its own, try the Chocolate-dipped strawberry recipe (see page 173), and increase your liquid intake at the same time.

"Twenty years ago a bagel was 140 calories and 7.5cm (3in) in diameter; today it has 350 and is 15cm (6in) in diameter."

Serving-size sprawl

Today's meals are "supersized," and we have become accustomed to seeing larger portions in restaurants. Unfortunately, this has translated into larger portions at home, too. For example, 20 years ago a fast-food hamburger was 333 calories; today it averages 590. Twenty years ago the average bagel was 140 calories and 7.5cm (3in) in diameter, while today it weighs in at 350 calories and is 15cm (6in) in diameter. This distortion in portion sizes is often why people gain too much weight.

Here are some analogies to help you visualize healthy portion sizes
- 85g (3oz) of meat is the size of a deck of playing cards
- 1 portion of potatoes, rice, or pasta is the size of a tennis ball
- 30g (1oz) of nuts is equal to a handful

Good portions come in small packages

You may be surprised at how many servings you are actually consuming – check the box on page 43 to find out. You can learn what a controlled portion of your favourite snack looks like by measuring it out the next time you eat it. Once you see what a serving really looks like, you'll be in no doubt about how much is too much.

minimizing weight gain

All women should gain at least 6.8kg (15lb) during pregnancy. It is not always easy to limit your weight gain to the recommended range. But of course you want to get your baby off to a healthy start by gaining the appropriate amount of weight.

You do need to increase your intake of most nutrients during your pregnancy, but gaining too much weight can cause you to give birth to a baby with a high birth weight, which means risk factors for health problems, such as obesity, heart disease, and diabetes, later in life. On the other hand, gaining less than the recommended amount can cause inadequate increases in maternal blood volume. This increases the risk of the baby having a low birth weight, which can lead to the baby having breathing difficulties, heart problems, and other complications, so don't go overboard with minimizing weight gain.

Filling up the healthy way

There are some tricks to filling up in a healthy way, which will prevent you from being tempted to fill out the wrong way:

- Load up your plate with lots of vegetables. This not only leaves you feeling more satisfied, it supplies you and your baby with extra nutrients and fibre without adding a lot of calories.
- Keep your portions moderate. Servings of beef, chicken, or fish should be 85–115g (3–4oz), which is not a very large amount.
- Always have some healthy snacks easily to hand and remove tempting foods from your home altogether. Slice up a selection of raw vegetables ahead of time and keep them in the refrigerator, so that when you get the munchies, you've got good food choices within easy reach. Keep a bottle of lowfat salad dressing or reduced-fat hummus for dipping.
- Drinking fruit juice in excess is a common mistake that women make in pregnancy. It is high in calories and sugar. It does contain nutrients, but you are much better off eating the whole fruit instead.
- Go for quality, not quantity, when you want to have a treat. Eat a piece of really good, high-quality chocolate instead of a whole chocolate bar – it will be just as satisfying and you will not be consuming so many calories.

SNACK ATTACK Have healthy snacks on hand at work to help keep hunger pangs at bay. If there are no high-fat, high-sugar snacks within easy reach, you won't be tempted by them.

LOW-CALORIE MUNCHIES

- Blueberries
- Carrot sticks
- Celery sticks
- Cucumber slices
- Fat-free yogurt
- Grapes
- Strawberries

Tips for increasing weight gain

Inadequate weight gain is most often a problem for women who are of low weight before pregnancy and is a risk factor for having a small or premature baby. A good way to increase your calorie intake is to increase the number of meals you eat in a day as many women, especially in the third trimester, find eating a large amount of food can cause real discomfort. Instead, try having six or more smaller meals a day, and increase your intake of carbohydrates, since they tend to be digested more easily. You can also increase your intake of calorie-dense foods, especially those from healthy fats. Exercise is important, too, because it will help stimulate your appetite.

Try the following

- Add olive oil or canola (rapeseed) oil to potatoes, dips, vegetables, beans, and soups
- Add a slice of cheese to your hamburger or sandwich
- Grate Parmesan cheese onto spaghetti, pizza, and casseroles
- Add cheese to salads, soups, and chilli
- Drizzle olive oil onto bread and sprinkle nuts on salads
- Snack on nuts, dried fruits, and avocados

SERVING SIZES AND DINING OUT

Avoid buffets and smorgasbords – it is nearly impossible to practise portion control in such situations. Don't be afraid to ask in a restaurant if you can have a smaller lunch-sized entrée. If not, ask for a takeaway container when the food is served and immediately put some away for later. Here are some examples of serving sizes to help you out:

A serving of grains is equal to:
- 75g (2½oz) oatmeal
- 45g (1½oz) cold cereal
- 75g (2½oz) cooked pasta
- ½ an English muffin
- 1 slice of bread

A serving of vegetables is equal to:
- 60g (2oz) lettuce
- 85g (3oz) cooked vegetables
- 175ml (6fl oz) vegetable juice

A serving of fruit is equal to:
- 1 medium-sized piece of fresh fruit (apple, pear, peach, banana, orange)
- 85g (3oz) chopped, cooked, or canned fruit, for example apple sauce or fruit salad
- 175ml (6fl oz) fruit juice

A serving of dairy is equal to:
- 240ml (8fl oz) milk or yogurt
- 45g (1½oz) cheese

A serving of meat or beans is equal to:
- 60–85g (2–3oz) cooked lean meat, poultry, or fish
- 85g (3oz) cooked beans
- 125g (4½oz) tofu
- 75g (2½oz) soya or veggie burger
- 1 egg
- 2 tablespoons of peanut butter
- 45g (1½oz) nuts

WHO SHOULDN'T EXERCISE?

Some women should not exercise in pregnancy. These include women with
• heart or lung disease
• an incompetent cervix
• persistent second- or third-trimester bleeding.

exercise

For too long we have told pregnant women to eat for two and limit their activities. This has contributed to obesity. Pregnancy is not a state of confinement – pregnant women are healthy and vibrant, and most can exercise vigorously.

The fact is, exercising while you are pregnant will improve your health generally, help you manage your weight, and ease the aches and pains that can accompany pregnancy. Exercise has no impact – positive or negative – on your baby. But, of course, a baby will certainly benefit from having a healthy mother.

Pregnant women with no medical or obstetric complications can follow the advice given most adults, which is to get at least 30 minutes of moderate exercise on most days of the week. Just be sure to listen to your body, and if you feel dizzy or very short of breath, stop exercising. As long as you are properly hydrated, the body heat generated by moderate exercise is no threat to your baby.

"Exercise has no impact – positive or negative – on your baby. But a baby will certainly benefit from having a healthy mother."

Exercising sensibly

Staying active during pregnancy is the best way to keep your weight gain within a healthy range. Of course, there are a few adjustments you need to make to ensure a safe routine of physical activity during pregnancy. Here are a few tips:
• Avoid hot tubs or saunas. Your circulatory system is already working hard enough pumping a greater volume of blood around your body while you are pregnant. The heat from the sauna or hot tub will cause your heart to work even harder, and you may possibly faint.
• Avoid exercise that risks abdominal impact in the second and third trimesters. Such activities include football, hockey, and basketball, and sports with a fall risk, such as skiing, rollerblading, and horse riding.
• During the second and third trimesters, do not exercise while lying flat on your back. This compresses the inferior vena cava blood vessel, and limits blood flow to the foetus. This applies to certain positions in weight training, yoga, and Pilates, so if you do take up these types of activities, find an instructor certified in pre-natal training.
• There is no data clearly showing harm from intense exercise. Still, be cautious and don't exercise to exhaustion. It makes sense for women who train hard during pregnancy to be monitored more closely by their obstetricians.

GENTLE EXERCISE If you are doing yoga or Pilates, for example, while you are pregnant, talk to your instructor about exercises that are safe and suitable.

One of the issues that women worry about most when they are pregnant is how much weight they will put on. It's important to stay fit and healthy, putting on the right amount weight for you, as an individual. This chapter has given you lots of information about the dos and don'ts of putting on weight in pregnancy and the checklist below provides a quick summary to refresh your memory if you are uncertain about something.

In summary...
how much weight?

1 **You need 200 calories more** every day while you are pregnant (in the third trimester). Gaining the correct weight will help get your baby off to a healthy start.

2 **Never skip meals in pregnancy** If you don't replenish your energy supply regularly, you'll find yourself low on energy and even light-headed.

3 **Don't feel you have to focus** on your week-to-week, or even month-to-month, weight gain. Just keep your target weight goal in mind.

4 **To prevent yourself becoming overweight** later in life, eat moderately, stay active, and be careful not to gain too much weight in pregnancy.

5 **Don't count calories,** but pay attention to portion sizes. When dining out, avoid supersized portions, all-you-can-eat buffets, and other excessive meal deals.

6 **Load up your plate with lots of vegetables** This not only leaves you feeling more satisfied, it supplies you and your baby with extra nutrients and fibre.

7 **To maximize weight gain** if you are underweight, have six or more smaller meals a day, and increase your intake of carbohydrates.

8 **Exercising while you are pregnant** will improve your health generally, help you manage your weight, and ease any aches and pains.

9 **Avoid hot tubs or saunas,** exercise that risks abdominal impact in the second and third trimesters, and exercising while lying flat on your back.

10 **Fruit juice is high in calories and sugar,** so keep your intake to a minimum. It does contain nutrients, but you are better off eating the whole fruit instead.

MANAGING YOUR WEIGHT

What's right for you?

To help you manage your weight gain most efficiently during your pregnancy you need to be familiar with what type of metabolism you had before you became pregnant:

• If you have a very rapid metabolism, you need to increase your daily intake of nutrient-rich, healthy foods to compensate for the rate at which you burn energy.

• If you have a slow metabolism and are concerned about putting on too much weight, it is perfectly safe to exercise to help keep your weight gain within the correct range.

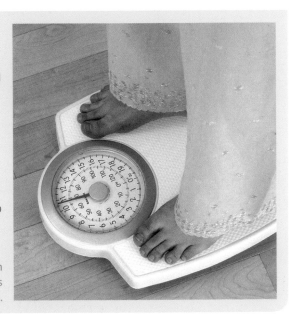

Everyone gains weight in a slightly different way in pregnancy. Keep your target weight in mind, but don't obsess about week-to-week or month-to-month weight gain.

first trimester

The first trimester is a vitally important time in your baby's development, because the foundations for all of your baby's major organs – the brain, heart, circulatory system, lungs, reproductive organs, and bladder – are now forming. Starting from a tiny speck of cells, the foetus becomes recognizable by the end of the first trimester. Your own body is changing dramatically, too, and for many women, the first trimester can be a physically trying time.

"Starting from a tiny speck of cells, the foetus becomes recognizable by the end of the first trimester."

Your body

The first trimester offers you windows of opportunity to maximize your baby's development, along with your own health and well-being, through diet and lifestyle. In the first stages of pregnancy, even before you have gained any weight, you will notice many changes. The earliest signs include nausea, breathlessness, and bloating, and you may also feel sleepy – some women sleep 12 hours at night and still take a 2-hour nap if they can. The hormonal changes that come with pregnancy may cause your breasts to swell and feel tender as the milk glands multiply. Such hormones also cause an increase in oil secretions from your skin, and many women get acne. Your growing uterus will begin to press on your bladder, causing frequent trips to the loo. Some women have no symptoms at all, however, and feel wonderful.

Outwardly, your body is minimally changed. But the small line in the positive pregnancy test, indicating the presence of the pregnancy hormone HCG (human chorionic gonadotropin) in your bloodstream, means that big changes are going on. Your heart rate and blood volume are increasing and will be 10–15 percent higher by the end of the first trimester at 12 weeks. This expansion requires extra fluid in your diet, as well as extra iron and folic acid. As blood volume increases, you may start to notice your veins more, particularly in your tummy, breasts, and legs. Your breasts and uterus are enlarging, and this growth requires extra protein in your diet. If this is your first pregnancy, you're probably not showing yet. However, you will tend to show earlier in subsequent pregnancies since your muscles and ligaments won't be so tight.

from egg to baby

You ovulate on approximately day 14 of your menstrual cycle. The egg that is released from your ovary is viable for about 24 hours, and if sperm make it to the Fallopian tube during this time, fertilization occurs. Starting as the two cells from the egg and the sperm, the embryo then divides, grows, and travels down the Fallopian tube.

By four days after ovulation, the embryo is made up of about 16 cells, and it enters the uterus. The cells attach themselves to the endometrial lining of the uterus, and are fully implanted within about three days. By the seventh day after conception, the embryo, called a blastocyst, is made up of 100 cells. Starting at this point, the human chorionic gonadotropin (HCG) becomes detectable in a blood test, and by two weeks after ovulation is also detectable in a home pregnancy test.

FOLATE-RICH CASHEWS During the first few weeks of pregnancy, when the foetus is no more than a collection of cells, one in five embryos miscarries. However, having sufficient folate in your diet may help make a chromosomally normal embryo less likely to miscarry.

Nature knows best

Many early embryos spontaneously miscarry during the first weeks of pregnancy. In fact, one in five pregnancies ends in miscarriage, which is nature's natural selection process. This is a sort of survival of the fittest, and little that you do will have any effect, because most of these were abnormal pregnancies from the start. Chromosomally normal embryos may be less likely to miscarry if you have adequate folate in your diet, but bear in mind that there are many other causes of miscarriage, too.

Hunger and nausea

In the early stages of pregnancy, your body needs about 100 extra calories daily, and you may feel hungry often, or nauseated as morning sickness kicks in. By week 7 or 8 about three-quarters of women find nausea a constant companion any time of the day, despite being called "morning" sickness. Your fluid requirements have increased, so be sure to drink lots of water to keep hydrated, especially when the vomiting is severe. By week 10, the nausea may ease a bit. By week 12, your uterus shifts up and forwards as it grows. The good news is it won't be pressing on your bladder so much and those loo visits will get less frequent. Enjoy this stage while you can, because by the third trimester the uterus will grow large enough to sit on your bladder once again. Morning sickness is usually getting better by this time, and you may be feeling less tired. However headaches and light-headedness are common now because of the increased blood volume.

In the first trimester, the foetus will develop everything from vital organs to limbs. The heart is the first organ to form, starting soon after the egg is implanted in the uterus, and fully functioning a few weeks later. The early spinal cord of the embryo

"By week 12, your uterus shifts up and forward as it grows. It won't be pressing on your bladder so much and those bathroom visits will get less frequent."

begins as a flat region, which rolls into a tube (the neural tube) four weeks after conception. Within this trimester, the fetus will have grown from a speck barely visible under the microscope to 8cm (3⅛in) in length, weighing about 45g (1.5oz).

By week 6 the embryo is about the size of a kidney bean. It has arm and leg buds, and the beginnings of all major organ systems. The brain begins its rapid growth. Now you can maximize the neural and brain development of your baby by getting plenty of omega-3 fatty acids in your diet (see page 27 for suggestions).

By 8 weeks, the embryo resembles a tiny human with the beginnings of eyespots, ears, and small arms and legs with tiny fingers and toes. As the nervous system becomes more interconnected, the foetus begins to move about. The placenta begins to form between 8 and 10 weeks. At this time your baby requires glucose as fuel, which you supply through your intake of carbohydrates. So you can feed your baby well by feeding yourself healthily. Carbohydrates are broken down in your bloodstream into glucose and pass through the placenta into your baby. Your blood and the baby's blood never mix because of the presence of a thin membrane between your circulation and the placenta. The exchange of oxygen, other nutrients, and waste products also takes place here.

DIETARY WINDOWS OF OPPORTUNITY

Brain and neural development

The foetus's brain and spinal cord develop from the neural tube, a structure that forms as a fold of tissue and, by six weeks after gestation, closes into a tube. If this tube does not close properly, the result can be severe birth defects, known as neural tube defects, which include spina bifida (openings in the spinal cord) and anencephaly (when most of the brain is missing and life is not sustainable). Depending upon where in the neural tube the defect occurs, the result can be mental retardation and/or paralysis. Studies show that a diet that includes adequate amounts of the B vitamin folate (or folic acid, the synthetic form of folate) can significantly reduce the incidence of neural tube defects. (For more information about folate and folic acid, see page 28.)

Getting the timing right

The closure of the neural tube is complete by six weeks following your last period, so it is important to ensure that you have adequate amounts of folate in your diet right away. Most women do not know they are pregnant until about one to two weeks after they miss their period, at the very earliest, and the neural tube finishes closing by two weeks after your missed period (six weeks after conception). It makes good sense to increase your intake of folate while you are trying to get pregnant.

Approximately 70 percent of all women of childbearing age still do not consume the recommended amount of folate, yet you can easily get enough from your diet if you are aware of good sources. To make absolutely certain that you have covered any possible time lag between conceiving and subsequently discovering that you are pregnant, either supplement your diet with folic acid, or be very aware of the folate content of all the foods you eat, to ensure that you are obtaining adequate amounts while you are still trying to conceive. The amount of folic acid needed to prevent neural tube defects is 0.4 milligrams (400 micrograms) of folic acid every day, the same as the recommended amount for all adults.

Sources of folate

Good sources of folate include green leafy vegetables (spinach, collards, Swiss chard, kale, mustard greens, turnip greens), legumes, nuts, and citrus fruits. Microwave cooking destroys more folate than any other cooking method, and it is also lost whenever high temperatures or large amounts of water are used in cooking. You can get folic acid from taking supplements or by eating breads and cereals fortified with folic acid. Some medications, including anticonvulsants, along with alcohol and cigarettes, may interfere with your ability to utilize folate or folic acid. This B-vitamin has been linked with a lower incidence of heart attacks, strokes, cancer, and diabetes, so everyone, not just pregnant women, benefits from increasing their intake of folate.

common ailments

Every trimester has its own characteristic impact on your body. The following list will help you learn what to expect and understand what is normal. It also has practical solutions for minimizing the effects.

Nausea

The hallmark of the first trimester, nausea, is what prompts many women to take a pregnancy test. Morning sickness, despite its name, can take hold at any time of day. Yet some pregnant women feel absolutely fine and are never nauseous. Others are incapacitated by it and even lose weight and require intravenous therapy. Nausea makes three-quarters of women feel ill, but does not affect their health or ability to carry on as normal. No one knows exactly what causes nausea or what is responsible for the different way it affects women.

Here's what we do know. The hormone progesterone slows down your gastrointestinal tract, so food sits in your stomach longer and moves more slowly through your system. The hormone HCG (human chorionic gonadotropin) is involved as well, because pregnancies that have high levels of HCG, such as twins or multiples, often come with a lot of nausea. But there is no consistent level of HCG at which women become nauseous. Two women can have the same HCG level and one will be nauseous, the other not. Finally, women with severe nausea have excellent pregnancy outcomes, even if they lose weight from it. Women with severe nausea have fewer miscarriages and pregnancy losses, and fewer pre-term deliveries. However, plenty of women with no nausea have a perfectly normal pregnancy – don't worry if you are not nauseous. The message is that if you are really nauseous, don't be

A PACKED LUNCH Depending on what you feel like eating, this may look more like breakfast than lunch. Anything you choose is fine, as long as it is nutritious and high in omega-3 fatty acids and folate.

CRYSTALLIZED GINGER Scientific evidence shows that eating ginger can diminish nausea after four days of including it in your diet. Either suck on crystallized ginger, grind up some fresh ginger into a lemon-ginger tea, or blend it into a nutritious smoothie.

overly concerned about it. It is very likely that, despite these trying times, you will be paid back for your suffering with a healthy pregnancy.

For some women, nausea and vomiting can be so severe that they become dehydrated, and need intravenous hydration, along with medication, but this is fairly rare. For most women, though, some simple dietary measures will do the trick. Nausea is usually worse if your stomach is empty, and better when you persistently eat a "white diet" of small amounts of bland carbohydrates such as pasta, rice, potatoes, and crackers throughout the day. Grazing on the white diet is often a good way to get through days when you are nauseous in the first trimester.

Breathlessness

Pregnancy hormones may have an effect on the respiratory centre of your brain, making you feel short of breath as early as the first trimester. You actually breathe at the same rate in pregnancy as in the non-pregnant state, but your respiratory mechanics change so you take deeper breaths. This allows extra oxygen to get to your baby. As pregnancy progresses, your diaphragm is pushed upwards by the enlarging uterus, and most women find the feeling of shortness of breath worsens. This is normal, and eating more frequent, smaller meals can make it a bit easier to breathe.

Breast tenderness

Most women notice breast tenderness almost as soon as they learn they are pregnant. This symptom can often be confused with the breast tenderness that accompanies premenstrual symptoms. Breast tenderness is usually the most noticeable with your first pregnancy, and tends not to be quite as noticeable in subsequent pregnancies. Your breasts may enlarge as early as the first trimester, and then naturally begin to lessen by the beginning of the second trimester. This decrease in breast tenderness, along with the lessening of nausea, often makes women worry they are no longer pregnant, but don't be fooled. It is natural to start feeling better by the end of the first trimester.

eating tips

For the busy woman in her first trimester eating may be a bit of a chore. You may not have much appetite, but with a little forward planning you can obtain all the nutrients you need.

Breakfast

You may not have much of an appetite in the morning in early pregnancy. You can get around this by planning your breakfast the night before so you don't have to think about it in the morning when you're rushed or only half awake. You don't have to limit yourself to traditional breakfast foods like toast, cereal, or eggs. One option is to pack a quick nutrient-rich healthy breakfast "to take away" the night before.

Snacks

Snacking in the first trimester is an important way to minimize nausea and maximize nutrition, and eating many small snacks spaced frequently throughout the day is a perfectly healthy way to eat. Choose bland carbohydrates if you are feeling poorly.

SMOOTHIES A great way to wake up your appetite, these highly nutritious, folate- and calcium-rich drinks (see recipes page 176) are only limited by your imagination. Use low-fat yogurt to minimize calories or full fat if you want to gain weight.

Eating lunch out

When dining out for lunch, it is helpful to ask the waiter for some altered preparations to cater to your altered palate. For example, you might like to order a pasta dish and ask for it to be tossed lightly with olive oil only and for the grated cheese to be put on the side. Order a plain baked potato that you put a small amount of butter or olive oil into. Avoid deep-fried foods and beef. A slice of plain cheese pizza may sit well with you, or you could try a cottage cheese and fruit plate. Salads may upset your stomach.

Dinner at home

Pasta or white rice with just a small amount of sauce, or a bit of butter or olive oil, is a good choice. Try White rice with red sauce (see page 143) or Couscous with olive oil and Italian parsley (page 133) to soothe your stomach. Mashed potatoes are often comforting. Try the recipe for Mashed potatoes with olive oil and fried garlic (page 134), but leave out the garlic in the first trimester. If you're not too nauseous, try Spaghetti with asparagus and toasted walnuts (page 144), for a burst of folate and omega-3 fatty acids.

Now that you know you really are pregnant, you can start getting used to your new state and eat accordingly. Your baby is developing fast and vital organs are forming. This summarization is intended to help keep you on track and to understand how to cope with the challenges of your pregnancy and your first trimester, in particular. If you are short of time this saves you from having to reread the entire chapter.

In summary...
the first trimester

1 **Evidence of change** Even though your body has changed very little from the outside this early in your pregnancy, huge changes are taking place within.

2 **Folate and folic acid** Even before you are pregnant, while you are still trying to conceive, increase your intake of folate or take a folic acid supplement.

3 **Nature knows best** One in five embryos miscarries very early. If possible, take heart in the fact that imperfect embryos miscarry spontaneously.

4 **Maximize development** The first trimester offers you the chance to maximize your baby's development, along with your own health, through your diet and lifestyle.

5 **Nauseous or not** Severe nausea (causing 10% body weight loss) or a total lack of nausea are not causes for concern. Both conditions still produce healthy babies.

6 Combat nausea Eating little and often, grazing on the "white diet," or consuming fresh or crystallized ginger can help combat nausea in the first trimester.

7 Breathlessness Eating small, frequent meals can help you cope with feelings of breathlessness, which are brought on by the changing hormones of pregnancy.

8 Calming of ailments If ailments, such as nausea and breast tenderness, fade away toward the end of the first trimester, it does not mean you are no longer pregnant.

9 Think ahead Planning and preparing breakfast the night before can make it easier for you to manage to eat breakfast, despite any nausea you might be suffering.

10 Specify your needs When dining out, phone ahead to make sure the restaurant is willing to prepare plain meals to your specifications.

EATING DINNER OUT

You may find eating dinner out in the first trimester is not the best idea. Often, as you get more tired, you get more nauseous. If you need to eat out to fulfill personal or business responsibilities, choose a restaurant that will serve you a plain pasta or rice dish made to your specifications, with just a bit of oil or butter and the cheese on the side. Try a plain piece of grilled chicken, and avoid beef or fish. A broth-based soup may be soothing, but stay away from creamy soups, which may upset your stomach. Don't give up on dessert. Just keep the portions small, or select fresh fruit.

This dish (Omelet with asparagus and Gruyère, see page 92) makes a lovely appetizer or main course. The eggs, cheese, and asparagus encompass a wide range of nutrients.

second trimester

The second trimester marks a wonderful time in pregnancy. Your energy increases, your taste buds return in full force, and you can begin to relish your role in helping to develop a healthy baby. Most of the difficult early symptoms are over (or soon will be) and your appetite returns. With it, however, come the notorious cravings of pregnancy.

"By the beginning of the second trimester you are noticeably pregnant, to yourself, and to everyone else."

Did you know that the three most common cravings in pregnancy are chocolate, salt, and fresh fruit? Luckily, you can quell your cravings in ways that are healthy yet still satisfying. If you are craving salt, you don't need to worry. You can salt your food to taste because you don't need to restrict your salt intake in pregnancy. Craving chocolate? Indulge in some fresh fruit dipped in antioxidant-rich dark chocolate (see recipe page 173). Small quantities of high-quality dark chocolate with cocoa levels of 70 percent or above can be a mood improver for both you and your baby. As well, studies show that women who consume chocolate during pregnancy have babies that show more laughing and smiling behaviour at six months of age.

By the beginning of the second trimester you are noticeably pregnant, at least to yourself, and to everyone else by the end. By 12 weeks you will have a visible bump, as the uterus rises out of your bony pelvis. But you are not so big yet that you are uncomfortable. For most women, the second trimester is a bit of a honeymoon period. Depending on your activity, your caloric needs in the second trimester are about 300–500 extra calories per day, and you need increasing amounts of calcium and iron.

In the second trimester, your hormones are leveling off. This means less nausea, you urinate less frequently, and suffer less exhaustion. What a relief! However, this is the time to be careful when exercising, to avoid falling and hitting your abdomen, so you will have to give up skiing, horseback riding, rollerblading, and contact sports. Otherwise, it is fine to exercise vigorously.

Here are some physical
changes you may notice:
• Veins on your chest and
breasts are dilated.
• Breast areolas may
darken and widen.
• The heart works harder,
pumping increased blood.
• Nasal stuffiness and
nosebleeds may occur due
to increased blood volume.

your body

As well as the general physical changes listed left, you may be noticing hormone-related skin changes. Some women develop the so-called "mask of pregnancy," blotchy patches with a darker pigment on your forehead, cheeks, nose, and chin. Itchiness is also common, and your skin may be dry and flaky, especially over your abdomen, where it is stretched. You can't prevent stretch marks, but lotions ease the dryness and itching. Staying hydrated will help ease the dryness, too.

Your uterus is just below your belly button by about 20 weeks. As your uterus grows, the ligaments supporting your uterus stretch, so you may feel some abdominal aches, and experience increased heartburn and constipation. The extra weight may begin to take its toll on your back, so wear low-heeled shoes and avoid sitting or standing for long periods of time. When you sit, use a footstool to raise your knees higher than your hips. If you become fatigued it is not uncommon to suffer from mood swings, too.

Your baby

The baby is looking more human each day. Usually the heartbeat is detectable by Doppler early in the second trimester, and the baby's gender is evident, but difficult to see by ultrasound until about the 16th week. By 12 weeks the foetal kidneys start to produce urine. Bones begin to form and the foetus will begin to draw calcium from your body. By 20 weeks the foetus bursts into action, kicking, bending, and making fists, stimulating the growth of muscles and joints.

The baby's central nervous system is now making connections to most parts of the body, allowing the brain to take control. Be sure to enrich your diet with omega-3 fatty acids to optimize this growth and development (see pages 20–37 for sources).

The digestive system matures now, and the foetus secretes insulin to let it take up glucose from the placenta. Your carbohydrates should come from unrefined sources, because refined starches and sugars will cause a high in the glucose level in your bloodstream. This will cross to the foetus, producing a peak of insulin to deal with the glucose load. Recent studies suggest this process may leave the foetus vulnerable to cardiovascular disease, diabetes, and obesity later in life.

POST-WORKOUT REHYDRATION
To avoid dizziness, light-
headedness or fainting, or to
replace fluids lost through
perspiration after a workout,
drink plenty of water. Eating
fruit makes a good snack to
take the edge off of any
hunger pangs, provide you
with fibre and nutrients, and
help you rehydrate at the
same time.

common ailments

Every trimester has its own characteristic impact on your body. The following list will help you learn what to expect and understand what is normal. It also has practical solutions for minimizing the effects.

Heartburn

Stomach acid normally stays in your stomach, but when it splashes up into your lower oesophagus it causes a burning sensation. Eating more frequent, small meals helps. Caffeine, peppermints, and chocolate can worsen heartburn. See for yourself what foods affect you. At night, lying flat can give you heartburn, so sleep propped up a bit, take an antacid tablet before going to bed, and try not to eat too close to bedtime.

Constipation

You need the extra fibre of whole grains, fruits, and vegetables to combat the natural slowing of your bowels at this time. Drinking extra fluids can keep your stools softer, as well as prevent the dreaded haemorrhoids. Drink water or seltzer with every meal and through the day. Caffeinated drinks tend to dehydrate you, so restrict them.

Dizziness

You may feel a bit dizzy when you go quickly from sitting to standing because your blood pressure is a bit lower. You can minimize such symptoms by staying hydrated. You can reliably judge for yourself how hydrated you are by looking at the colour of your urine (see above left). One of the best ways to get hydrated is to eat fruits that are high in water, such as strawberries, grapes, and melons.

Mood swings

Fatigue and hormonal changes can cause mood swings and symptoms similar to PMS. If you are having some ups and downs, try adding some sources of omega-3 fatty acids to your diet. Scientific findings indicate that these may improve mental health.

Hot flushes

You may now feel the heat in your body generated by the foetus and begin to notice hot flushes (similar to menopause) from hormonal surges. Dress in layers so that you can adjust to these swings in body heat, and stay well hydrated to lessen symptoms.

eating tips

For the busy woman in her second trimester eating may be more appealing than it was in the first. You'll wake up feeling like breakfast and enjoy snacks, too.

Breakfast

A good breakfast is even more important now, since the foetus is constantly drawing nutrients from your body. Avoid high-sugar choices, such as sweetened cereals or pastries. Choose fibre-rich food, such as a wholegrain cereal or wholewheat bread, a piece of fruit, and some protein, such as milk, cheese, yogurt, peanut butter, or eggs. Bananas make a quick and hearty part of a nutritious breakfast. Try the recipe for Ginger-vanilla yogurt with blueberries and bananas (page 101).

Snacks

BLUEBERRY AND CREAM-CHEESE STUFFED FRENCH TOAST A good breakfast can take only minutes to prepare. The most important meal of the day, it will keep you energized and stop you from overeating at lunch (see page 96).

Pregnant women often need to snack in the second trimester, and it is common to feel hungry between meals and possibly even during the night. Dried fruit and nut mixtures are nutritious snacks you can put in small bags and keep handy at home and on the go. All nuts are a great source of heart-healthy oils and supply you with vitamin E. Try to include walnuts in your diet during the second trimester, since they are rich in omega-3 fatty acids, which are important in your baby's current rapid brain growth. Dried fruits are rich in nutrients as well as fibre. Try several kinds, such as raisins, dried cherries, dried cranberries, dried figs, dates, wild blueberries, and apricots. A few dark chocolate chips for a bit of sweetness will calm your chocolate cravings and add an antioxidant punch.

Always keep a variety of fresh fruits on hand. Oranges, clementines, tangerines, grapefruit, and plums travel well, since they don't bruise easily. In the second trimester, virtually all vitamins, except vitamin A, are needed in larger amounts, and a variety of fruits will supply vitamins B (including folate) and C. Chopped vegetables, such as broccoli, cauliflower, celery and carrot sticks, as well as sliced red peppers, are delicious, refreshing, and packed with fibre. Add a bottle of salad dressing and have a vegetable and dressing snack. You can also dip the vegetables in hummus.

Aim for five servings of fruits and vegetables daily. The more servings you consume, the better, so feel free to indulge in many varieties. The more variety in your diet, the more likely you'll be to obtain the different nutrients you need.

Lunch

If you feel like a sandwich, choose turkey or roast beef, rather than more processed meats, such as baloney or salami, which are high in saturated fat and additives. Remember that listeria is a bacterium that can contaminate deli meats, so microwave deli meats until they are hot and steaming to ensure safety. Once they have been thoroughly reheated it is safe to allow them to cool before you eat them so you don't burn your mouth. Romaine lettuce, a good source of folate and calcium, goes well on sandwiches and stays crisp. Your baby's developing skeleton now needs increasing amounts of calcium, so add a slice of tomato for a bit of vitamin C and cheese for calcium.

LUNCH ON THE GO Your lunch hour may be far less than an hour. Plan ahead so that what you eat is nutritious and filling. Get as much variety into your meal as possible to obtain the widest range of nutrients. The selection above will give you a good lunch plus extra snacks to get you through your busy day.

Eggs make a great protein-rich part of your lunch. Look for omega-3-enriched eggs, which are eggs from hens that are fed flax seed. Omega-3 fatty acids help in neural development in your baby, which may make for a smarter baby. Hard-boil a few eggs, and put a pinch of salt on them. Add a few wholegrain crackers or a piece of wholewheat bread for an easy unrefined carbohydrate source, plus a piece of fruit, and all of your nutrient needs at lunch are covered.

Eating lunch out Salads are now a good option, because your taste buds and stomach can easily cope with a mix of greens and more. Choose interesting salads made with dried fruits, nuts, and seeds. Ask for the dressing on the side, and use only what you need to keep your calorie intake down. Pizza is a good choice, especially if you stick to vegetarian toppings. They are lower in fat than meat toppings and the vegetables offer added nutrients. To keep your refined carbohydrate intake low, always look for pizza restaurants offering a wholewheat crust as an option.

Salmon, which is featured on most restaurant menus, is a heart-healthy protein rich in healthy fats. It is a pregnancy superfood, and is safe because it is not high in mercury. Salmon is high in omega-3 fatty acids, which the rapidly growing foetal brain needs now. (Wild salmon has the highest amounts of omega-3 fatty acids.)

Dinner

The second trimester is a great time to experiment with a variety of strong and contrasting flavours, since studies show that your baby is more likely to try new flavours later in life having "tasted" them in the womb. Pay attention to your cravings because they are your body's way of signalling what it needs. You may crave red meat, which is rich in haem iron, a form of iron that is well absorbed. Now your taste buds are ready for fish again, so try the delicious recipe for Linguine with shrimp, tomatoes, and parsley (page 145). To bring back some bold flavours, try Chicken, corn, and black bean enchiladas (page 151), a recipe that can be prepared right out of your pregnancy pantry (see page 183). One of the most common cravings in pregnancy is salt, so instead of grabbing a bag of crisps when you walk in the door after a long day, try whipping up Salty Tuscan pork chops with caramelized apples and shallots (page 157). Spicy is probably second on your cravings list after salt, so try Spicy chicken breasts with an avocado-corn salsa (page 152).

Eating dinner out Eating out in the second trimester your options are wide, as long as you make good choices. Healthy eating does not necessarily mean giving up everything you love, so your meals can be delicious and indulgent. Choose foods such as legumes, grains, vegetables, and fruits, and avoid dishes with heavy batters or sauces. Go for grilled or poached fish rather than fish dipped in batter and fried.

"Healthy eating does not mean giving up everything you love, so your meals can be delicious and indulgent."

When ordering red meat, choose a lean cut that is roasted, or grilled. Avoid anything described as "buttery," "in butter sauce," "pan-fried," "crispy," "fried," "creamed," "in cream sauce," "hollandaise," "au gratin," or "escalloped."

Do not be afraid to ask your waiter questions about how things are prepared or to ask for all dressings and sauces to be served on the side so that you can control how much is added to your portion. Check to be certain no raw eggs or unpasteurized dairy products are being used.

To minimize your calorie intake and eat healthily, do not feel you have to finish everything on your plate. Limit the portion size of cooked meat, fish, or poultry to 115g (4oz). Trim all visible fat off meat, and remove skin from poultry. Limit yourself to one piece of bread and reduce the amount of olive oil or butter.

By the time you have arrived at the second trimester, you may well feel that you are getting used to being pregnant. Your pregnancy nausea, if you had it, will probably have ceased by now, and you'll feel you've got a lot more energy than before. Now is the time to take stock about what you are eating and all the other issues of your condition, so use this easy summary checklist to help remind you of this chapter's contents.

In summary...
the second trimester

1 **Smooth sailing** Most of the early symptoms of pregnancy are nearly gone, but you may now find yourself craving chocolate, salt or fresh fruit.

2 **Increased needs** Depending on your activities, you now need an extra 300–500 calories a day, plus increasing amounts of calcium and iron.

3 **Exercise caution** Be extra careful when exercising, to avoid falling and hitting your abdomen. Avoid skiing, horse riding, rollerblading, and contact sports.

4 **Fluid intake** Staying hydrated is more important than ever now to counteract constipation, feeling dizzy, light-headed, or faint, and to avoid dry skin.

5 **Handling heartburn** Eat small meals often, not too close to bedtime, sleep propped up, and take an antacid tablet to help ease the sensations of heartburn.

6 **Mood improvers** Depression may be reduced by consuming more omega-3 fatty acids and occasionally having a small piece of high-quality dark chocolate.

7 **Extra weight** Use a footstool when you sit to raise your knees above your hips to ease the strain on your back and help the circulation in your legs.

8 **Layered dressing** Wearing layers of clothing and drinking lots will help regulate your temperature now that the foetus's heat is giving you hot flushes.

9 **Dining out** Find out how food is prepared and ask to have any dressings or sauces served on the side in order to control your calorie intake.

10 **Handful of nutrients** Snacks of small portions of dried fruits and nuts are packed with nutrients and fibre – everything you need in this trimester.

LUNCH LOGIC

Winning combinations

The basic formula for the components of a healthy lunch is to eat a protein source, an unrefined carbohydrate source and a fruit or vegetable. Examples of combinations that fulfill this balance include:

• A few cubes of cheese, some grapes (or other fruit) and wholewheat crackers

• Yogurt sprinkled with muesli and dried fruit

• A salad (see right), made with tomato, lettuce (romaine contains folate and calcium) and some cheese and wholewheat bread

• Hard-boiled eggs, celery, and carrot sticks and wholewheat bread

• Left-over baked chicken pieces, with thin cucumber slices sprinkled with salt and a slice of wholewheat bread

• Wholewheat pitta bread with hummus, cucumber and tomato.

A crisp salad with a modest amount of dressing offers plenty of nutrients. The eggs, cheese and asparagus encompass a wide range of nutrients.

third trimester

Having a baby may seem more like a reality in the third trimester – you will soon get to see the baby whom you have worked so hard to keep healthy. This can be a physically trying time because your baby is growing larger and your body feels the strain, so it is more important than ever to eat well and take care of yourself and your baby. By leading a healthy lifestyle and eating a good diet, you can minimize your discomfort and maximize both your health and your baby's.

"Increasingly strong foetal movements that you are probably feeling are evidence that your pregnancy is reaching its natural conclusion."

What's happening in your body

The third trimester is a time of remarkable changes in your body. Your bulge protrudes noticeably as, on average, your baby approaches 3kg (7lb) by the time he or she is born, and the volume of your amniotic fluid reaches just under 1 litre (33fl oz). Your placenta usually weighs in at about one-tenth the weight of the baby. Add to this the fact that your blood volume is 50 percent higher than when you started pregnancy, and your tissues contain several pounds of fluid – small wonder that you are feeling the strain. Very little of the weight you've accumulated is actually fat, however. This lean body gain comprises your baby, placenta, amniotic fluid, blood volume, breast enlargement, and fluid in your tissues. By the time you reach term, only about 1.8–2.2kg (4–5lb) of your weight gain is fat, and you'll draw on those fat stores when you breastfeed to supply your baby with nutrition in the newborn period.

The discomforts of pregnancy may take centre stage in the third trimester, as the uterus takes up more and more room inside you. Backaches, urinary symptoms, heartburn, constipation, fatigue and sleep disturbances can all become more common. But the increasingly strong foetal movements you are probably feeling are evidence that your pregnancy is reaching its natural conclusion.

what's happening

By 25 weeks, towards the end of the second trimester, the baby's bony skeleton is fully assembled and it is from then until you give birth that your dietary calcium needs are greatest. Even if you do not obtain adequate calcium at this time, the foetus will draw it from the reserves in your skeleton regardless.

The third trimester is also the time when the foetal brain and nervous system undergo their most dramatic growth and development. According to studies, if you eat a diet rich in omega-3 fatty acids (see page 27 for sources) you will nourish and maximize your baby's neural and brain development, as well as intelligence, and minimize developmental disorders later in life.

Iron supplies

In addition to the calcium the baby draws from you, which its skeleton needs in order to mineralize in the third trimester, it will now draw the most iron from your blood supply. Take care of your iron needs because the baby will obtain all the iron it needs from you, even if you do not get enough in your diet; it could be at your expense if you don't. Emphasize iron-rich foods (see page 28) and combine these with foods or beverages rich in vitamin C, such as some orange juice, to maximize your absorption of iron. You need to try to avoid becoming anaemic, which could leave you run down when the time comes to deliver, and after the birth, too.

Weight gain

The baby is gaining weight fast, so you need more calories, too; about 200 extra a day, just during the third trimester. A normal baby weighs about 3.4kg (7½lb) at birth. Your diet plays a role in achieving this weight, so most women should gain 11–15.8kg (25–35lb). If you are overweight, limit your weight gain to 6.8kg (15lb), and if you are underweight, increase your gain to 18kg (40lb) (see page 40). Staying within normal weight gain ensures your baby achieves genetic growth potential, yet minimizes the risk it will be born bigger than is healthy, a possible risk factor later.

Ultrasound scans frequently show that unborn babies stick out their tongue. The baby's mouth and nose are filled with amniotic fluid, which carries the tastes and smells of the mother's diet. The baby's mouth is full of taste buds, so it is possible that the baby might be tasting the amniotic fluid. We know the mother's diet may influence the taste and odour of amniotic fluid, so indulge in some new and varied tastes in the third trimester, and let your baby taste them too. (Studies show that women who drink carrot juice while pregnant have toddlers who are more likely to accept drinking carrot juice.)

By the third trimester, you'll feel your baby move many times each day. You may also feel the baby hiccuping. These involuntary diaphragm contractions are a sign of good health, so don't be concerned about them.

EASY-GOING MEALS No matter how busy you may be, try to relax while you eat as this will promote good digestion and therefore optimum absorption of the nutrients that you and your baby need.

common ailments

Every trimester has its own characteristic impact on your body. The following list will help you learn what to expect and understand what is normal. It also has practical solutions for minimizing the effects.

Swelling

Swelling is normal, and different women swell to varying degrees. It is only a problem if you also have high blood pressure, so this is a good way to differentiate worrying swelling from what is normal. It is extra important to drink lots of fluids, since it can be harder to stay hydrated when fluid in your bloodstream is leaking into your tissues.

Constipation

Almost 90 percent of pregnant women develop constipation, most commonly in the third trimester, so make sure you drink a lot of water and eat fibre-rich foods, such as fruits, vegetables, and wholegrains (see pages 30–31 for sources). Minimizing constipation will also keep away the dreaded haemorrhoids (varicose veins of the rectum), which are common in pregnancy even if you are not constipated.

Reduced bladder capacity

Your uterus is now pressing right up against your bladder, decreasing its capacity. You may find that you urgently run to the loo, only to realize you have just a small amount of urine to release. Pressure from the uterus also causes the bladder to leak occasionally when you laugh, sneeze, or cough. The best way to combat this problem is to practise Kegel exercises. These are done by tightening the muscles supporting your pelvic zone as though you were stopping a flow of urine. Hold for a count of eight. Then repeat in sets of 10 several times throughout the day.

Fatigue

As you get close to term, you'll find your energy levels decreasing. It takes a great deal of energy to make a baby, and that, combined with the interrupted sleep of the third trimester, for example due to getting up to pass urine frequently in the night, makes for tiredness. Combat this with energizing meals rich in unrefined carbohydrates, such as brown rice, wholegrain cereals, wholewheat pasta and wholegrain breads.

"It takes a great deal of energy to make a baby, and that, combined with interrupted sleep, makes for tiredness."

CARROT JUICE As well as keeping you hydrated, carrot juice is rich in calcium and iron, of which you need a lot in your third trimester. While you want to stay hydrated in pregnancy, you can minimize night-time urination interrupting your sleep by not drinking too much after suppertime.

eating tips

For the busy woman in her third trimester, eating may seem a little tricky at times. You are hungry, and then cannot finish what you start. But small, high-quality, nutrient-dense meals will see you through.

Breakfast

Constipation is such a common problem in the third trimester that a good way to get your day off to a great start is with a fibre-rich wholegrain cereal. Enrich it with extra nutrients and fibre by sprinkling on dried fruit, nuts, ground flax seed, or wheatgerm. If you are trying to gain weight, use whole milk, and if you are trying to minimize weight gain, use skimmed milk. You will not be doing yourself any harm if you skip fruit juice at breakfast altogether (see left).

On the weekends, relax and enjoy a leisurely breakfast. If you're troubled by constipation, whip up some Hearty hot oats with dried fruit and nuts (see recipe page 95). If you're craving salt, try Spanish-style eggs with potatoes, onion, and spicy sausage (see recipe page 93), and use eggs enriched with omega-3 fatty acids to enhance your baby's rapid brain development during the third trimester.

Snacks

The key to comfortable eating in the third trimester is frequent small meals with snacks in between. You will likely have a good appetite at each meal, but then quickly get full and uncomfortable.

Steam some fresh broccoli and keep it in your refrigerator, or chop it up and keep it raw, and serve it with a dipping sauce. A great snack, it is rich in iron, folate and fibre, to serve all your third trimester needs.

Scones also make a terrific snack. Whip up a large batch, wrap them individually and freeze them. Try the Dark chocolate dried-cherry scones (see recipe page 121). They'll satisfy that craving for chocolate and give you antioxidant health benefits.

Lunch

Lunch on the go Pack a lunch to take to work in the third trimester – you're not going to get the high-quality nutrition you need if you eat out regularly. Wholewheat rollups with tangy white beans and vegetables (see recipe page 114) are a great choice. Make the filling ahead and refrigerate it, so you can save time later.

LOSE THE JUICE Limit yourself to a 90–120ml (3–4fl oz) glass of fruit juice a day now. You are much better off eating the whole fruit because fruit juice is high in sugar and the sugar high can be followed by a sugar low an hour later, leaving you light-headed.

"When you arrive home from work you may be tired and hungry and…oh my…craving salt."

Eating lunch out You'll want to make wise choices when you do decide to have the occasional lunch out during the third trimester. Restaurant portions tend to be larger than you'll feel comfortable finishing, so don't be afraid to leave some behind, and don't hesitate to ask to take home a doggie bag for your supper. Choose light meals such as soup, salad, or simple pasta or rice dishes. Too much heavy food at lunchtime will leave you snoozing at your desk by the middle of the afternoon.

Dinner

Quick suppers When you arrive home from work, you may be tired and hungry, and …oh my…craving salt. Salt is a common craving in pregnancy, and luckily, you don't need to restrict salt despite what your mother may have told you, so go ahead and salt freshly prepared foods to taste. Satisfy that craving, along with your hunger, with a speedy supper that you can make once a week and that the whole family is sure to enjoy. Salty Tuscan pork chops with caramelized apples and shallots (see recipe page 157) will please everyone. Serve the pork chops with a side of fresh vegetables, such as spinach or broccoli, a piece of crusty bread, and dinner is served. In this delicious yet simple supper, the sweet apples cut the saltiness of the pork a bit. To save time in the evening, the apples can be prepared a day in advance and refrigerated, but bring them to room temperature before serving. If you have more time, accompany the meal with Mashed potatoes with olive oil and fried garlic (see recipe page 134).

If you are very tired, you can always put together some super-quick, throw-together, no-cook dinner solutions out of the pregnancy pantry (see page 175). For example, take a wholewheat tortilla, sprinkle it with shredded Cheddar cheese, add 85g (3oz) drained and rinsed tinned beans, spoon on some ready-made salsa, and microwave it until hot for a quick burrito. Or try some cheese chunks, fruit and mixed nuts for a meal that you can even eat in bed, if you want.

Eating dinner out You may find that you want to have dinner out once in a while as a treat in the third trimester, but make it an early one. As you get further into the third trimester, you'll be very fatigued by the end of the day, and sitting for long periods of time may make your back ache. Be sure to choose restaurants that have speedy service and comfortable chairs. Emphasize fresh simple meals such as grilled fish or chicken, or go vegetarian and let someone else do all the vegetable chopping. Avoid refined carbohydrates by substituting brown rice for white rice, sweet potatoes for white potatoes and wholewheat pasta for white.

Now you have reached the third trimester, your baby is getting large and will be more of a reality to you. The strain of moving around may be great, so now is the time to get as much rest as you can, lead a healthy lifestyle, and also to eat as well as you possibly can. The points listed below are a summary of this chapter, so use it as a quick refresher to remind yourself of the main points made.

In summary...
the third trimester

1 **Keep up the good habits** Minimize discomforts and maximize your and your baby's health by continuing to lead a healthy lifestyle and eat a good diet.

2 **Nearing the end** You may often be uncomfortable now, but the strong foetal movements you are feeling mean your pregnancy is reaching its natural conclusion.

3 **Nutritional resources** Your baby is drawing heavily on your stores of calcium and iron. Keep your intake of these high so you do not become depleted yourself.

4 **Vary your foods** Babies in the womb stick out their tongue and taste the amniotic fluid. Eat a variety of foods to introduce the baby to new tastes.

5 **Normal swelling** Every pregnant woman swells to some degree and it is only considered a problem if you have high blood pressure.

6 **Fibre** Keep your fibre and fluid intake high now to counteract constipation and avoid haemorrhoids, which are a common problem in pregnancy.

7 **Bladder control** Inhibit bladder leakage by doing Kegel exercises every day and drink lots earlier in the day to avoid interrupting your sleep to urinate during the night.

8 **Energy output** Broken sleep and the energy it takes to make a baby will fatigue you in your third trimester, so eat energizing unrefined carbohydrates.

9 **Small meals** You may start off hungry but be unable to finish your food, so the key to comfortable eating in the third trimester is small, frequent meals and snacks.

10 **Homemade** To get the high-quality nutrition you need now, make your own meals to take with you, so you can control exactly what is in them (see below).

MAKE AND TAKE

Keeping track of nutrient content

During the third trimester you need to keep your intake of iron and calcium very high because the baby is drawing on your reserves. If your iron levels are low you can become run down and anaemic (see page 28 for dietary sources of iron) and if you are depleted of calcium you may suffer from hypertensive disorders (see page 29 for calcium sources). In the third trimester, it is more important than ever that you know exactly what you are eating, so take the time to prepare your foods ahead and take them with you.

This Dark chocolate dried-cherry scone (see page 121) makes a good breakfast or snack. It contains a variety of nutrients and will fill you up without making you feel uncomfortable.

postpartum

It's wise to plan ahead for the first few whirlwind days after delivery. If you're reading this at the end of your third trimester, take the opportunity to make preparations to ensure you get optimum nutrition during the important time right after your baby is born. It's useful to have prepared lists of meals you are going to cook and fresh ingredients to shop for, and to have a fully stocked pregnancy pantry.

> "Since you are physically and emotionally depleted, the postpartum period is an important time to nourish both body and mind."

The first two weeks

Was that not a miracle? The initial days of postpartum recovery can be a mix of joy and pain, euphoria and exhaustion. Since you are physically and emotionally depleted, it is an important time to nourish your body and mind. Sleep is your number one priority. Many women sleep poorly in the weeks preceding delivery, and labour often lasts through at least one night, so most women and their partners are sleep deprived when their baby finally arrives. Try to rest while recovering in the hospital or at home right after the birth, and limit visitors to one part of the day so you can nap. Your nights are likely to be interrupted with feedings, so napping is one of the keys to survival in the first few weeks postpartum. Learn to sleep when your baby sleeps. Many newborns are nocturnal, so you may be keeping some very irregular hours.

It is time to restore your body's stocks of nutrients. Enjoy some unrefined carbohydrates, which will give you the sustained energy you need. Your body is healing, so be sure to have adequate protein in your diet to aid this process. Include a protein source (beef, chicken, fish, dairy, beans, or nuts) in all three of your meals, and you'll almost automatically get enough. Hydration is also essential. Dramatic fluid shifts occur during delivery and postpartum, and most women actually have more swelling in the first week after giving birth. This will naturally go away, and you should be certain to continue drinking fluids and eating water-rich fruits to stay hydrated. Constipation is a very common problem postpartum. Most women dread their first bowel movement, but take heart – often the anticipation is worse than the event.

- apple slices spread with peanut or almond butter
- apple sauce
- baby carrot sticks dipped in hummus
- celery sticks spread with cream cheese
- dried fruit
- flavoured rice cakes
- fresh fruit
- nuts
- slice of wholegrain bread with peanut butter, cheese, or sardines
- smoothies (see page 176)
- Steamed broccoli with a divine dipping sauce (see page 118)
- sunflower seeds
- Sweet potato-pecan bread (see page 119)
- wholewheat pretzels
- wholewheat tortilla wraps with cream cheese and vegetable slices

what to eat

In those first few days, putting nutritional advice into practice can be a challenge. Hormone swings can trigger cravings for sugar and unhealthy foods. Some mothers give up on food preparation completely during this time, indulging these cravings and subsisting on takeout or ready-made packaged meals that do not meet their nutritional needs.

However, it is important to eat foods that replenish nutrients now to give yourself the quickest recovery and minimize your risks for anaemia and postpartum mood swings. You have probably just lost up to about 5.5kg (12lb) – 2.2kg (7lb) of baby, 0.9kg (2lb) of placenta, and 1.3kg (3lb) of blood and amniotic fluid. It will take a while for the rest of your weight to come off, so don't try to rush the weight-loss process.

Breakfast

A good breakfast can consist of one or two hard-boiled eggs enriched with omega-3 fatty acids with wholewheat toast, or wholegrain cereal with fresh fruit or a dollop of yogurt. Don't rule out having soup for breakfast, because a steaming bowl of vegetable, beef, chicken, or fish soup with a warm chunk of wholegrain bread can be nourishing and soothing. Smoothies make a great hot-weather breakfast.

Lunch and dinner

Salads are excellent meals or components of meals. Simply mix and match the ingredients kept in your refrigerator. Start with torn pieces of lettuce and add cheese chunks, bean sprouts, chilled steamed asparagus or broccoli, drained and rinsed canned beans, and hard-boiled eggs. Slices of avocado are a tasty addition, and are rich in healthy fats. Top your salad with pumpkin or sunflower seeds and vinaigrette made from balsamic vinegar. Add a slice of crusty wholewheat bread drizzled with olive oil and your meal is complete. A hot sandwich makes a great lunch or dinner, so try the Turkey sausage and broccoli rabe sandwiches (see page 113). The Baguette pizzas (see page 116) make perfect quick postpartum meals. Wholewheat rollups with tangy white beans and vegetables (see page 114) are a good choice, since the bean mixture can be prepared several days ahead. Egg dishes make great lunches or dinners. Try the Swiss chard and feta frittata (see page 117).

Postpartum and breastfeeding diet

The diet for women in the postpartum period, whether or not you are breastfeeding, is based on the same healthy formula that was set in place during pregnancy. Breastfeeding women need 200–500 calories more a day, and slightly more protein (about 70g/2oz per day), and should increase portion sizes to accomplish this. Other than this, you don't need to change the basic balance of protein, carbohydrates, and fats you ate while pregnant. Breastfeeding women should also be extra vigilant about hydration, and drink about eight 175–240ml (6–8oz) glasses of fluid every day to offset the fluid losses from breast-feeding. Stick with the same formula you used in pregnancy:

- 50–60 percent of your calories from carbohydrates
- 25–35 percent from fat
- 20 percent from protein (70g/2oz per day)

HEALTHY SNACKS Snacks are as crucial as naps in the postpartum period. Frequent feeds for your baby can make it difficult for you to eat enough meals, so snacking is key. If you are breastfeeding, snacking is doubly important, because only you can feed the baby. Choose healthy, nutrient-rich snacks that you can keep beside you while you are breastfeeding.

Crucial calcium

You need 1,000mg of calcium a day when you are breastfeeding (see page 29 for sources). Studies have shown that women often lose 3–5 percent of their bone mass during breastfeeding, although it is rapidly recovered after weaning. Just be sure to get adequate calcium and vitamin D during and after breastfeeding.

Omega-3 fatty acids

Studies suggest that breastfed babies may have an intelligence boost, due to omega-3 fatty acids in the mother's diet. The newborn baby's brain is rapidly developing, and these fatty acids seem to continue to aid it in its healthy formation. There is also data that daughters of mothers who breastfeed and have a diet rich in these fatty acids may have lower risks of developing breast cancer later in life. Finally, omega-3 fatty acids are great for the mother's health, too, because recent studies suggest that they may decrease the risk for postpartum depression.

FIT IN MEALS WHEN YOU CAN
In the early days, lunch and dinner are pretty well interchangeable. Your meals need to be quick to prepare, satisfying, and easy to eat on the run. Mozzarella muffin melt (see page 100 for recipe) makes a quick and healthy light meal any time of day.

Hydration

It is important that breastfeeding mothers drink enough fluids. Your baby will breastfeed up to 8–12 times a day, so you may need up to 3 litres (5¼ pints) of fluid a day just to compensate for the breast milk your baby is drinking. A good method to keep up with your fluid needs is to have 250ml (8fl oz) of fluid at each breastfeeding session. Don't wait until you are thirsty, since this means you're already dehydrated. If your urine is dark and has a strong smell, it means you're not drinking enough.

Vitamins and supplements

You can meet all of your needs in breastfeeding with a healthy diet. However, sometimes eating a healthy diet can be a challenge when you are taking care of a newborn. Taking a pre-natal vitamin or a multivitamin while breastfeeding can be a method of insurance against any nutrient deficits. You may need an additional calcium supplement to meet your calcium needs, especially if you are restricting dairy products, for example, due to allergy in yourself or potential allergy in your baby (see Infant food sensitivity, opposite). It is not a good idea to limit dairy products as a means of losing weight. Instead, choose non- or low-fat dairy products. The calcium is not contained in the fat, so removing it leaves the calcium behind. Remember, you can't make up for a poor diet with a vitamin, but you can fill in some gaps.

Foods to avoid

Some of the restrictions you practised while pregnant are now loosened, but others still apply to breastfeeding. For example, the restriction on seafood still holds, since any mercury in seafood can get into your breast milk, and can damage your newborn's brain. The restriction on foods that may contain listeria is no longer an issue in breastfeeding, since listeria infects the placenta, which is no longer present.

Mercury Studies have shown higher levels of mercury in the breast milk of mothers who eat large amounts of fish. Mercury levels in breast milk are about one-third the level of mercury in the mother's blood, so if you are breastfeeding, carry on avoiding the same fish you did when you were pregnant (see page 35).

No one completely understands colic, but you probably know it when you have a colicky baby. Colic can be more specifically defined by episodes of inconsolable crying that:

• Begin within the first three weeks of your baby's life.
• Last at least three hours a day.
• Occur at least three days a week.
• Continue for at least three weeks.
• Rarely last longer than three months of age.

Infant food sensitivity

Nothing is easier for an infant's stomach to digest than breast milk. However, some breastfed babies seem to react to foods their mothers eat. Remember, it is normal for breastfed babies to have loose stools and be occasionally irritable, so be cautious about jumping to conclusions. Infant food sensitivity does occur, but is not common and is a controversial area; studies estimate that 3–7 percent of babies suffer.

Infant food sensitivity can be one of the triggers of colic, and making some changes in your diet, in partnership with your paediatrician, can help in some cases. The most common offender with sensitivity and allergy is cow's milk, which contains a protein that can be difficult for some babies to digest. Some women are able to continue eating yogurt and cheese, while cutting back or eliminating milk. If you are limiting your intake of dairy products, be sure to take a calcium supplement.

Peanut problems

Peanuts are one of the most common causes of food allergy, and in some, peanut allergies can cause severe reactions. Your baby may be at higher risk of developing a peanut allergy if you, the baby's father, brothers, or sisters have a food allergy, or if other allergic conditions such as hay fever, asthma, and/or eczema run in the family. If your baby is in this higher-risk group, you may wish to avoid peanuts and peanut products while you're breastfeeding and while you're introducing solid foods.

Alcohol and caffeine

It's a good idea to keep your alcohol and caffeine intake on the moderate side. The ideal time to drink alcohol is just after you breastfeed, rather than just before. Alcohol clears the breast milk in about the same time it takes to clear your bloodstream, so you may want to wait six to eight hours before breastfeeding again. Alcohol does not go into your milk and stay there. If you feel fine, then most of the alcohol is out of your milk and you can nurse. If you have any doubt, pump and dump the breast milk once and that should eliminate any traces of alcohol.

The amount of caffeine that makes it into your milk is only about 1 percent of the level in you, so the level in your breastfed baby's blood will also be low but will eventually accumulate. Studies show that up to five caffeinated beverages per day are acceptable. Make sure to count all sources of caffeine, such as tea, soft drinks, pain relievers, and chocolate. If you consume more than five servings of caffeine a day it may collect in your baby's system, resulting in wakefulness and irritability. To be prudent, it is best to limit caffeinated beverages to two cups per day.

It is safe and healthy
to exercise while
breastfeeding. Studies have
shown no difference in the
volume or composition of
the milk or the babies'
weight gain. Most studies
have found no difference in
acceptance of the breast,
even after intense exercise.
There is no reason to wait
to feed after exercising.
• For your own comfort,
you may wish to feed
before exercising; breasts
that are full of milk can be
heavy and uncomfortable.
Wear a good supportive bra.
• Some babies don't like
feeding when mum has
been sweating (due to the
salt on mum's skin), so you
may wish to rinse your
breasts or take a shower
before feeding.
• If you regularly lift
weights or do other
exercises involving
repetitive arm movement
and you develop plugged
ducts, cut back and start
again more slowly.
• Most importantly,
remember to keep yourself
very well hydrated.

getting your body back

The best way to lose weight postpartum, or really any time, is to practise portion control by eating foods in smaller quantities. Too much of any food, no matter how healthy, will cause you to gain weight.

If you're breastfeeding

However, do not to be overly restrictive in your caloric intake because while breastfeeding, you should consume a minimum of 1,800 calories a day. Very low-calorie diets can adversely affect your milk production and leave you exhausted. Your intake does not need to be absolutely precise in order for your baby to have adequate nutrition, and even if your diet is not perfect, the nutrient content of your milk is still generally preserved. But eating a poor-quality diet, or a diet with insufficient calories, on a regular basis may leave you feeling fatigued from eating improperly.

If you stick to your healthy pregnancy diet, you'll likely lose weight while breastfeeding, since it burns up a lot of calories. But most breastfeeding women feel extra hungry. Pay attention to what you eat so you can lose weight in a manner that is healthy for you and your baby. Some women lose weight quickly in the first month, especially if they have retained extra fluid. After this time, it is safe to lose weight at a rate of 0.9kg (2lb) a month without affecting the breast-milk volume you supply your baby. If you began your pregnancy overweight, an acceptable weight loss is 1.8kg (4lb) a month.

If you are not breastfeeding

Don't rush to start dieting after giving birth. For the first six weeks, concentrate on healthy eating, and developing an exercise plan. Then, when your body has begun to recover and your periods have returned to normal, follow a healthy weight-loss plan. A healthy rate of weight loss is 1.8kg (4lb) monthly.

Exercise

Moderate exercise – about 30 minutes of physical activity per day that gets your heart pumping and leaves you slightly breathless – enhances general health, weight loss, weight maintenance, and mental health. It's good for your heart, strengthens your body, energizes you, helps clear your fuzzy postpartum head, and may help you sleep more soundly, even during those short hours between feeds.

GET MOVING! You can start going for walks immediately after either a normal or a Caesarean delivery. After a normal delivery, you can gradually build up to more strenuous exercise on an "as you feel up to it" basis. Listen to your body, and if you have pain slow down. After a Caesarean delivery you need to wait until you have clearance from your physician before you take on more strenuous exercise.

"Very low-calorie diets can adversely affect your milk and leave you feeling fatigued from eating improperly."

After the whirlwind of the birth, the mixtures of emotions and the adjustments to your new life with a baby, now is the time to take stock and concentrate on getting enough sleep and the right kind of food. This summary, which picks out the main points in the chapter, will help you keep on track and enable you to cope with the challenges of the postpartum phase. If you are short of time, which is very likely, this saves you from having to reread the entire chapter.

In summary...
postpartum

1 **Plan ahead** Make lists, and prepare and freeze meals to reheat and enjoy during the whirlwind early days of caring for your newborn baby.

2 **Get enough sleep** Make it a priority to get as much sleep and as many naps as you can whenever possible, to build up your energy levels and help your body heal.

3 **Flexible mealtimes** You must eat whether you are breastfeeding or bottle-feeding. If there's no time for sit-down meals, eat frequent nutritious snacks.

4 **Nutrient-rich foods** Your hormones may trigger cravings for sugar and unhealthy foods, but you need proper nourishment to aid recovery and keep you strong.

5 **Breastfeeding** You need 200–500 calories more a day if you are breastfeeding, plus extra fluids to replace those lost through breast milk.

6 **Strength in variety** By varying your diet you can expose your baby to new taste sensations through your breast milk.

7 **Taking supplements** If you find eating a balanced diet difficult at this busy time, take multivitamin and calcium supplements to fill in the gaps.

8 **Food restrictions** Continue to follow fish guidelines for pregnancy (see page 35), since mercury can pass in your breast milk to your baby.

9 **Alcohol in moderation** Drink alcohol after you have breastfed and wait for it to pass out of your system before you nurse again.

10 **Get out of the house** Walking is the best exercise after giving birth and offers a number of benefits to you and the baby.

EXPOSING BABY TO NEW FLAVOURS

Just as in pregnancy, when amniotic fluid may be flavoured, experts feel that one advantage to breastfeeding may be that the milk is flavoured by the foods the mother eats, so babies become used to a variety of taste sensations. One famous study showed that when mothers ate a diet rich in garlic, their milk tasted and smelled like garlic. Not only did the babies who drank the milk not have any digestive problems, they actually preferred the garlicky milk to the unflavoured milk. Eating a variety of foods while you are breastfeeding gives your baby a more adventurous diet.

This Black bean and bulghur salad with parsley and lemon (see page 127 for recipe) is packed with goodness, plus a range of tastes to pass on to your baby through breast milk.

the recipes — eating for two

It's easy to eat well in pregnancy. This section is packed with delicious breakfasts, lunches and dinners and snacks and treats, too.

cooked breakfasts

It's been said many times, but breakfast really is the most important meal of the day. Skipping breakfast is like starting on a car journey with your petrol tank almost empty. You're bound to run out of fuel halfway through a busy morning. Use your pregnancy as an opportunity to adopt healthy habits that will benefit both you and your baby throughout your lives. Eating breakfast is a great way to start this new regimen, and a hot breakfast is a particularly good choice.

Studies show that breakfast-eaters are healthier because they take in a better mix of nutrients and have a much higher intake of vitamins and minerals than those who skip this meal. This is because breakfast foods themselves provide a variety of nutrients, and because non-breakfast-eaters are more apt to snack throughout the day, often on unhealthy foods. Starting your day with a healthy breakfast sets the stage for good food choices as the day progresses and leads to fewer food cravings.

In pregnancy a good breakfast is even more important. Without the right morning jump-start, you may feel weak, lethargic, or nauseated during the day, because your baby is constantly drawing on your glucose stores for its own needs. The baby will do this whether or not you meet your own nutritional needs. When you don't, you will quickly feel the lack of energy.

Skipping breakfast is no way to minimize weight gain in pregnancy. It will only result in overeating at lunchtime. In fact, studies show that breakfast is an important key to weight management, and not just for a mum-to-be. A good breakfast actually helps you eat fewer calories over the course of the day. Eating breakfast also benefits intellectual energy and performance, at work and school. So as a pregnant woman, it is of paramount importance that you start off the day right, for you and your baby.

asparagus and gruyère omelette

rich in: ✓folate ✓calcium

When you have a morning to enjoy a leisurely breakfast, this omelette is the perfect dish to make. It is rich in folate from the asparagus, which contains more of this nutrient than any other vegetable, and healthy protein from eggs. In addition, the cheese offers an excellent source of calcium to build your baby's bones and teeth.

Preparation 15 minutes
Cooking 5 minutes
Makes 2 servings

225g (8oz) fine asparagus spears
2 eggs
3 egg whites
1 tbsp reduced-fat single cream
¼ tsp sea salt
freshly ground black pepper to taste
15g (½oz) unsalted butter
60g (2oz) Gruyère cheese, sliced or grated

1 Bring 300ml (10fl oz) of water to the boil in a small frying pan or other wide pan. Add the asparagus spears, cover, and steam for 3–5 minutes until tender. Drain in a colander and rinse under cold running water. Set aside.

2 Lightly beat together the eggs, egg whites, cream, salt, and black pepper in a small bowl. Melt half of the butter in a small non-stick frying pan over a medium heat. When the butter has stopped foaming, raise the heat slightly and pour half of the egg mixture into the pan. Cook the eggs for about 10 seconds until they begin to bubble around the edges. With a fork, gently lift an edge of the omelette and allow the liquid egg to run onto the hot pan. Lift another edge and repeat the procedure.

3 When the base of the omelette is set but the top is still a bit wet, spread half of the steamed asparagus and Gruyère over one half. Fold the other half of the omelette over the asparagus and cheese, and cook for a further 1 minute. Remove from the pan and keep warm while you cook a second omelette in the same way. Serve hot.

RECIPE NOTES
• Broccoli florets can be substituted for the asparagus.
• Serve with hearty multigrain toast and a virgin Bloody Mary for a real Sunday treat.

spanish-style eggs with potatoes, onion, and spicy sausage

rich in: ✓ carbohydrates ✓ protein

Craving savoury tastes? Satisfy this in a healthy way by adding some zesty sausage to eggs and make a Spanish tortilla, which is a flat omelette like the Italian frittata. You'll get an energy boost from this carbohydrate- and protein-rich breakfast.

Preparation 5 minutes
Cooking 15 minutes
Makes 2 servings

2 tbsp olive oil

1 medium baking potato, about 300g (10oz), peeled and cut into 1cm (½in) cubes

½ tsp sea salt

1 small onion, diced

115g (4oz) spicy or herby pork sausages, removed from the skin and crumbled

4 eggs, beaten

1 Heat 1 tablespoon of the olive oil in a 25cm (10in) non-stick frying pan over a medium-high heat. When the oil is hot, add the potato cubes and sprinkle them with ¼ teaspoon of the salt. Sauté, tossing occasionally, for about 5 minutes until the potatoes are golden and soft. Transfer them to a plate and set aside for a moment.

2 Add the remaining tablespoon of oil to the pan. When it is hot, add the onion and sausagemeat. Cook, stirring occasionally, for about 5 minutes until the onion is soft and the sausage is browned and crumbly. Return the potato cubes to the pan and mix the ingredients together well, then spread them out in the pan.

3 Pour the eggs into the pan and sprinkle with the remaining ¼ teaspoon of salt. Let the eggs set for 1 minute, then lift the edge of the eggs all around and tilt the pan so that the uncooked egg can run onto the hot surface. Let the eggs set for another minute. Repeat the lifting and tilting procedure again.

4 Turn a large plate upside down and place it on top of the pan. Holding the plate close to the pan, invert the pan so that the omelette falls out onto the plate. Slide the omelette back into the pan, uncooked side down, and cook for a further 1–2 minutes. Remove the pan from the heat. Cut the omelette in half and serve at once.

RECIPE NOTES
• This flat omelette is equally good at room temperature.
• If your frying pan is suitable for use under the grill, rather than turning the omelette out onto a plate, leave it in the pan and cook the top under a hot grill.
• To make a lower-calorie version, substitute 3 egg whites for 2 of the eggs.

eggs and cheddar with salsa and corn tortillas

rich in: ✓ protein ✓ calcium

This makes a great Sunday brunch dish. Studies show that exposing a baby to a variety of flavours while in utero may enhance his or her acceptance of new foods later in life. So add some piquant salsa to your scrambled eggs, to begin building your baby's palate.

Preparation 10 minutes
Cooking 20 minutes
Makes 4 servings

4 corn tortillas, 15cm (6in) in diameter

60g (2oz) mature Cheddar cheese, grated

4 eggs

4 egg whites

¼ tsp sea salt

15g (½oz) unsalted butter

1 avocado, peeled, stoned, and sliced

30g (1oz) fresh coriander, chopped

Salsa

1 tbsp olive oil

2 garlic cloves, thinly sliced

1 small onion, diced

1 jalapeño or other green chilli, or to taste, seeded and finely chopped

¼ tsp sea salt

½ tsp ground cumin

½ tsp chilli powder

4 canned plum tomatoes, drained and chopped

1 Preheat the oven to 150°C/Gas 3. Spread out the tortillas on a baking tray. Divide the cheese among the tortillas, scattering it over them evenly. Place the tray in the oven and heat the tortillas for about 10 minutes until they are soft and the cheese has melted.

2 Meanwhile, prepare the salsa. Heat the olive oil in a saucepan over a medium heat. Add the garlic and cook for about 45 seconds until soft and fragrant. Add the onion and chilli. Sprinkle the ingredients with the salt and cook for about 5 minutes until soft, stirring often. Stir in the cumin and chilli powder, and cook for 1 more minute. Raise the heat to high and stir in 250ml (8fl oz) water. Simmer for 1 minute. Add the tomatoes and simmer for a further 3 minutes, stirring occasionally. Remove the pan from the heat and set aside.

3 Beat together the eggs and egg whites, and season with the salt. Melt the butter in a frying pan over a medium heat. When the butter stops sizzling, add the eggs and cook until soft curds form. Lift them away with a fork and tilt the pan so that the uncooked eggs can flow to the bottom. Continue cooking the eggs in this manner until they are firm but the top is still moist. Remove the pan from the heat.

4 To assemble the dish, divide the warm tortillas among 4 plates. Place a few avocado slices around the edge of each tortilla, spoon the eggs into the centre, and top with salsa. Garnish the tortillas with the coriander and serve at once.

RECIPE NOTES
• If you are in a hurry, substitute your favourite ready-made salsa for the salsa here.
• Instead of scrambling, you can poach or fry the eggs.

hearty hot oats with dried fruit and nuts

rich in: ✓ fibre ✓ carbohydrates

This is not only delicious, it is a triple fibre feast from the oats, dried fruit, and nuts. The hormone progesterone slows down bowel motility, so most pregnant women have some trouble with constipation. A breakfast like this is a great way to get you moving.

Preparation 5 minutes
Cooking 25 minutes
Makes 4 servings

60g (2oz) slivered almonds

½ tsp sea salt

175g (6oz) steel-cut Irish oatmeal

6 dried apple rings, coarsely chopped

6 dried apricots, coarsely chopped

75g (2½oz) raisins

skimmed milk for serving

maple syrup for drizzling

1 Place the almonds in a small frying pan over a low heat. Toast them, shaking the pan occasionally, for about 8 minutes until they are golden.

2 Meanwhile, bring 2.4 litres (4 pints) water to the boil in a heavy saucepan. Add the salt, then slowly stir in the oatmeal. When the water comes back to the boil, reduce the heat and simmer the oatmeal for 20 minutes, stirring occasionally, or according to packet instructions. Stir in the dried apples, apricots, and raisins. Cook the oatmeal for 5 more minutes.

3 Divide the oatmeal among 4 shallow bowls. Thin each portion with skimmed milk. Drizzle with maple syrup, garnish with the toasted almonds, and serve at once.

RECIPE NOTE

• For a richer and higher-calorie version, substitute whole milk for the skimmed milk.

tip *Constipation may be a problem in the third trimester, when your growing uterus impairs motility of your intestines. Combat this with a fibre-rich diet.*

blueberry and cream cheese-stuffed french toast

rich in: ✓antioxidants ✓fibre

Using wholemeal bread and adding blueberries turns traditional French toast, or *pain perdu*, into a very healthy and delicious breakfast. Of all fruits, blueberries have the highest content of antioxidants, which have a host of health-promoting properties for both you and your baby.

Preparation 20 minutes
Cooking 15–20 minutes
Makes 4 servings

150g (5½oz) thawed frozen or fresh blueberries

225g (8oz) extra light low-fat soft cheese or fromage frais (see Food precautions, page 35)

4 eggs

4 egg whites

120ml (4fl oz) skimmed milk

4 tbsp honey

8 slices wholemeal bread, 1–2 days old

60g (2oz) unsalted butter

250ml (8fl oz) maple syrup for serving

4 tbsp toasted flaked almonds

1 Stir together the blueberries and cream cheese in a bowl. Set aside.
2 In a shallow bowl that is large enough to hold 4 slices of bread side by side, whisk together 2 of the eggs, 2 egg whites, 4 tablespoons of the milk, and 2 tablespoons honey. Dip 4 slices of bread into the egg mixture and soak for 5 minutes. Flip the slices over and soak for another 5 minutes. Transfer the soaked slices to a plate. Repeat the procedure with the remaining eggs, whites, milk, honey, and bread.
3 While the second batch of bread slices is soaking, heat a large frying pan or griddle over a medium heat. Add half of the butter to the pan. When it stops sizzling, add the first batch of bread slices. Raise the heat slightly and cook for about 3 minutes until the base of each slice is golden. Flip the bread over and cook for a further 3 minutes.
4 Divide half of the blueberry mixture between 2 of the slices, spreading it out evenly. Cover with the other 2 cooked slices to form 2 sandwiches. Remove them from the pan and keep warm. Repeat the cooking and stuffing procedures with the remaining soaked slices of bread, butter, and blueberry filling.
5 Divide the sandwiches among 4 plates. Drizzle 4 tablespoons maple syrup over each sandwich, sprinkle with the toasted almonds, and serve at once.

RECIPE NOTES
• For a higher calorie version, substitute single cream for the milk and use regular soft cheese instead of low-fat.
• Your favourite berry or combination of berries, whole or sliced, can be substituted for the blueberries.
• To speed up the preparation and cooking, use 2 shallow bowls and 2 frying pans.

quick breakfasts

More than one-third of young adults skip breakfast. You're too busy. You're trying to watch your weight. You don't have time to make toast, much less eggs and bacon. However, just 10 minutes of munching can sustain you for hours on end. Breakfast serves up a good dose of key nutrients that you and your baby need: calcium from milk; vitamin C and folate from fruit; and fibre from wholegrain cereals and breads. So do yourself and your baby a favour. Make time for breakfast.

You can follow a few simple principles to make certain your breakfast gets you off to the best possible start:
• Include a fibre-rich food, such as a wholegrain cereal or wholemeal bread.
• Include a piece of fruit.
• Include a source of protein, such as milk, cheese, yogurt, peanut butter, or eggs.
• Avoid high-sugar choices such as sweetened cereals or pastries.

Use your imagination to put together something quick. Remember, breakfast does not have to include traditional breakfast foods. Here are a few ideas to get you started:
• frozen wholegrain waffles quickly toasted and topped with sliced strawberries and Greek yogurt or half-fat crème fraîche
• a Galia or Ogen melon half filled with cottage cheese
• the previous evening's dinner wrapped in a wholegrain flour tortilla
• a wholemeal bagel spread with low-fat soft cheese or fromage frais and topped with sliced apples and raisins
• granola or muesli stirred into vanilla yogurt, topped with sliced strawberries or raspberries and a drizzle of maple syrup
• sliced bananas topped with vanilla yogurt, drizzled with honey, and sprinkled with coarsely chopped walnuts and raisins or other dried fruit of your choice.

mozzarella muffin melt

rich in: ✓ **fibre** ✓ **calcium**

What could be quicker than melted cheese on a toasted muffin? Pop this in the oven when you are getting dressed, then wrap it in a paper napkin and head out of the door. By choosing a wholemeal muffin, and having a piece of fresh fruit too, you'll get all you need for a healthy yet incredibly speedy breakfast.

Preparation 5 minutes
Cooking 10 minutes
Makes 1 serving

1 wholemeal muffin, split open

1 medium tomato, sliced

60g (2oz) mozzarella cheese, sliced

sea salt to taste

fresh basil leaves or finely chopped fresh flat-leaf parsley to garnish (optional)

1 Preheat the oven to 200°C/Gas 6. Place the muffin halves, cut side up, on a small baking tray. Divide the tomato slices and cheese slices between the halves and sprinkle with a little salt.

2 Bake for about 10 minutes until the cheese has melted and the muffin is slightly crisp. Serve immediately, garnished with basil or parsley if you like.

RECIPE NOTES

• Cheddar or Gruyère cheese can be substituted for the mozzarella.

• Instead of tomato slices, try frozen chopped spinach that has been thawed, squeezed to remove excess moisture, and seasoned.

• If you prefer, you can heat and toast the cheesy muffins under a medium grill.

tip *If you are feeling nauseous during the first trimester, bland cheese such as mozzarella is a good choice. Later, when you are feeling better, substitute Cheddar or another strong cheese.*

ginger-vanilla yogurt with blueberries and bananas

rich in: ✓ calcium ✓ antioxidants

Start your day off right with this quick fruit and yogurt treat. The ginger gives it a flavour punch and will also help quell your nausea. Yogurt is a great source of calcium, and blueberries are one of the richest fruit sources of beneficial antioxidants.

Preparation 10 minutes
Cooking none
Makes 2 servings

250g (9oz) fat-free vanilla yogurt

2.5cm (1in) piece fresh ginger, peeled and finely chopped

1 medium banana, peeled and cut into chunks

150g (5½oz) blueberries

8 tbsp granola (home-made, see page 104, or ready made)

1 Place the yogurt, ginger, and banana in a blender. Turn the blender on and process the ingredients until smooth.
2 Divide the yogurt mixture between 2 dessert glasses or bowls. Garnish each with blueberries and granola, and serve immediately.

RECIPE NOTE
• If you are trying to gain weight, substitute whole-milk yogurt for the fat-free yogurt.

tip *Bananas taste great for breakfast and their health benefits are truly astounding: rich in vitamin B$_6$ and a good source of fibre, vitamin C, magnesium, and potassium.*

breakfast burrito

rich in: ✓ fibre ✓ protein

This vegetarian burrito makes a great quick breakfast. The filling of tofu, scrambled eggs, and cheese is wrapped in a wholemeal flour tortilla, along with sliced avocado and chopped tomatoes. Tofu is rich in fibre and protein, and avocados are rich in fibre and healthy fats. It's a super way to start your day.

Preparation 15 minutes
Cooking 10 minutes
Makes 2 servings

115g (4oz) firm tofu

3 eggs

3 egg whites

½ tsp sea salt

freshly ground black pepper to taste

15g (½oz) unsalted butter

115g (4oz) Cheddar cheese, grated

4 wholemeal flour tortillas, 25cm (10in) in diameter

1 ripe avocado, peeled, stoned, and sliced

1 large tomato, cored and diced

1 To remove the excess moisture from the tofu, you need to press it. Place it on a large plate, set another plate, right side up, on top, and place a heavy pan on top of the second plate. Let the tofu drain for 15 minutes, then discard the collected liquid. Crumble the tofu and set it aside.

2 Whisk together the eggs, egg whites, salt, and black pepper in a bowl. Melt the butter in a frying pan over a medium heat. When the butter stops foaming, add the egg mixture and cook until soft curds form. Lift them up with a fork and tilt the pan so that the uncooked egg can flow onto the bottom. Continue cooking the eggs in this manner until they are firm but the top is still slightly moist. Remove from the heat and stir in the crumbled tofu.

3 Divide the cheese among the tortillas, spreading it out evenly. Microwave each tortilla for about 30 seconds until the cheese melts and the tortillas are warm.

4 Divide the egg and tofu mixture among the tortillas. Garnish each with avocado slices and diced tomato. Fold in the sides, then roll up each tortilla from the bottom to enclose the filling completely. Serve immediately.

RECIPE NOTES
• To save time, press the tofu a day in advance.
• You can replace the tomato with your favourite home-made or ready-made salsa.

bountiful bagel sandwiches

rich in: ✓ fibre ✓ carbohydrates

These bagels may not have traditional morning flavours, but for pregnant women craving strong tastes, they could be just right. Wholegrain bagels are a great way to begin your busy day, since the unrefined carbohydrates will give you sustaining fuel for the entire morning, and they are a terrific source of fibre.

Preparation 10 minutes
Cooking 5 minutes
Makes 2 servings

2 wholegrain bagels
150g (5½oz) low-fat soft cheese
1 carrot, peeled and grated
2 spring onions, trimmed and thinly sliced
1 tomato, sliced
1 small cucumber, sliced

1 Slice the bagels open in half and toast them.
2 While they are toasting, combine the soft cheese, carrot, and spring onions, mixing them together well.
3 Spread an equal amount of the soft cheese mixture on the cut side of each bagel half. Top each with a slice of tomato and a couple of cucumber slices, and serve.

RECIPE NOTES
• You can substitute 4 slices of wholegrain bread for the bagels.
• The soft cheese mixture can be prepared a day in advance and refrigerated.

tip *Substituting low-fat for regular soft cheese removes some of the saturated fat, yet retains all the protein and calcium. The same is true for other dairy products, such as cheese, yogurt, and milk.*

nutty granola

rich in: ✓ fibre ✓ antioxidants

Beware of ready-made granolas that claim to be healthy – many contain large amounts of sugar and fat. It's much better to make your own granola, to enjoy as a quick and satisfying breakfast with milk or yogurt, as well as a fibre-rich snack, ideal for munching in the early days with your newborn, when you have only one hand free!

Preparation 5 minutes
Cooking 20 minutes
Makes 8 servings

125g (4½oz) rolled oats

60g (2oz) walnuts, coarsely chopped

75g (2½oz) unblanched almonds, coarsely chopped

50g (1¾oz) sesame seeds

good pinch of sea salt

25g (scant 1oz) toasted wheat germ

75g (2½oz) light soft brown sugar

½ tsp ground cinnamon

140g (5oz) dried cranberries

1 Heat a large, heavy frying pan over a medium-low heat. Add the oats, walnuts, and almonds. Toast them, stirring often, for about 6 minutes until they begin to colour. Add the sesame seeds and continue toasting for 5 minutes, stirring often.

2 Stir in the salt, wheat germ, and brown sugar. Continue cooking the granola, stirring constantly, for about 1 minute until the sugar has melted. Reduce the heat to low and stir in the cinnamon and dried cranberries.

3 Transfer the granola to a large baking tray and spread it out to cool. Once it is cold, store the granola in an airtight container, where it will keep for up to 1 week.

RECIPE NOTES

• Mix your bowl of granola with milk and top with fresh blueberries.

• Sprinkle some granola on vanilla yogurt along with sliced strawberries and add a drizzle of honey.

• Once the granola is cold, stir in a handful of dark chocolate chips – dark chocolate is a rich source of antioxidants.

• Substitute pecan nuts or cashews for the walnuts or almonds.

• Add 1–2 tablespoons of ground linseed (flax seed) to the cooled granola.

light meals and snacks

For many women, light meals and snacks are the perfect way to eat during pregnancy. Early on, you may find that an empty stomach makes you feel nauseous, yet a big meal makes you uncomfortable. Known as the "white diet" for the pregnant woman, snacks such as water biscuits, rice, pasta, potatoes, and other bland foods are ideal when you feel queasy. Later, as your growing uterus takes up more space, it is common to get full very easily, especially in the third trimester.

Most pregnant women feel hungry about every 3 to 4 hours, yet once you sit down to a meal you often feel too full to finish, and pushing yourself to eat more can make you very uncomfortable. Frequent small meals and snacks are a good solution.

Sandwiches and wraps make great fast, light meals, eaten sitting down or on the go. Choose flavourful sandwich breads and tortillas that contain fibre, such as multigrain, wholemeal, bran, or oats. Add lettuce, tomato, and other vegetables, such as cucumber, red peppers, or carrots, for taste and crunch. On their own, fruits, vegetables, and toast are all great snacks.

Keep in mind that the time to try to lose weight is before, not during, pregnancy. Most of the weight you gain in pregnancy is in fact lean body gain. By term, only about 1.8–2.25kg (4–5lb) of the total amount of weight that you gain is fat. You need to increase your daily calories to gain this healthy weight, which go towards building your baby, your uterus, your breasts, and your blood supply.

You can keep weight gain to healthy norms by eating light meals, and then have healthy snacks in between meals to offset your hunger. Your snacks should not be equivalent to a full meal – just simple foods to get you through until your next meal.

stir-fried pak choy and sweet peppers with roasted tofu

rich in: ✓protein ✓fibre ✓folate

This dish looks as beautiful as it is delicious, and it may convince even the most ardent meat-eaters to become vegetarian. In addition to protein, nuts are a great way to add fibre and folate to any meal. This dish also contains plenty of ginger, which can diminish nausea.

Preparation 20 minutes
Cooking 15 minutes
Makes 4 servings

450g (1lb) extra-firm tofu
2 tbsp tamari or soy sauce
1 tbsp caster sugar
4 tbsp sesame seeds
1 tbsp canola (rapeseed) oil

Stir-fried vegetables
1 tbsp canola (rapeseed) oil
2.5cm (1in) piece fresh ginger, peeled and thinly sliced
1 red pepper, cored and cut into strips
450g (1lb) broccoli, separated into florets
350g (12oz) pak choy, stalks sliced into 2.5cm (1in) pieces and leaves chopped
3 tbsp black bean sauce
75g (2½oz) unsalted cashews, coarsely chopped

1 To remove the excess moisture from the tofu, you need to press it (see page 102).
2 Preheat the oven to 200°C/Gas 6. Cube the tofu and place it in a shallow bowl. Add the tamari and sugar to the tofu and gently toss to combine. Sprinkle with the sesame seeds and toss well. Spread the canola oil on a baking tray. Scatter the tofu cubes onto the tray in a single layer. Roast the tofu for about 15 minutes until golden.
3 Meanwhile, stir-fry the vegetables. Heat the canola oil in a wok over a high heat, then add the ginger and cook for 30 seconds. Quickly add the red pepper, broccoli florets, and pak choy stalks. Stir-fry the vegetables for 2 minutes.
4 Add the pak choy leaves and 250ml (8fl oz) water. Continue to stir-fry for 1 minute. Add the black bean sauce and stir-fry for another minute.
5 Transfer the stir-fry to a large platter. Scatter the chopped cashews and tofu cubes on top and serve at once.

RECIPE NOTES
• Black bean sauce is available with or without garlic.
• The stir-fry can be served with steamed white or brown rice or tossed with Chinese egg noodles.

broccoli and cheddar-stuffed potatoes

rich in: ✓ calcium ✓ fibre

Try this in the second and third trimester, as well as post partum, when you need extra calcium and fibre. This dish gives you a double dose of both nutrients – calcium from the broccoli (one of the best vegetable sources) and cheeses, and fibre from the broccoli and potatoes.

Preparation 15 minutes
Cooking 1¼ hours
Makes 4 servings

4 large baking potatoes, scrubbed

olive oil for rubbing

550g (1¼lb) broccoli, separated into florets

450g (1lb) low-fat cottage cheese

1 large tomato, cored and diced

250g (9oz) Cheddar cheese, grated

1 tsp sea salt

freshly ground black pepper to taste

1 Preheat the oven to 200°C/Gas 6. Pierce the skin of each potato 3 or 4 times with a fork, then rub them with olive oil. Bake for 45–60 minutes until they are tender.

2 Meanwhile, bring 5cm (2in) of water to the boil in a saucepan. Stir in the broccoli. Cover the pan and steam the broccoli for about 5 minutes until it is bright green and just tender. Drain and rinse under cold running water. Set aside.

3 When the potatoes are done, remove them from the oven. Leave the oven on. Carefully slice each potato in half lengthways and allow them to cool slightly. Scoop the flesh from the potato halves into a bowl, taking care not to tear the skins. With a fork, mash the potato flesh. Stir in the cottage cheese, diced tomato, just over half of the Cheddar, and the cooked broccoli florets. Season the mixture with the salt and some black pepper.

4 Divide the mixture among the hollowed-out potato halves. Sprinkle with the remaining Cheddar. Return the potatoes to the oven and bake for about 10 minutes until they are heated through and the cheese has melted. Serve hot.

RECIPE NOTES

• Replace the broccoli with spinach sautéed with garlic in olive oil. Or add your own favourite vegetables.

• The potatoes can be baked and stuffed a day in advance, then refrigerated. Since they will go into the oven cold, they'll need about 25 minutes to bring them to hot serving temperature.

• Make some extras, because the potatoes will reheat very well in the microwave for a busy weeknight supper.

sesame tofu with orange-ginger broccoli

rich in: ✓ protein ✓ calcium ✓ fibre

A vegetarian diet is healthy in pregnancy, and tofu provides a great vegetarian protein source. Broccoli is a super vegetable, being rich in calcium and fibre. This dish is easy to make – most of the time is for pressing and marinating the tofu, which can be done the night before.

Preparation 50 minutes
Cooking 15 minutes
Makes 4 servings

450g (1lb) extra-firm tofu
2 tbsp tamari or soy sauce
120ml (4fl oz) orange juice
½ tsp sea salt
4 tbsp sesame seeds
1 tbsp canola (rapeseed) oil

Broccoli
750g (1lb 10oz) broccoli
1 tbsp canola (rapeseed) oil
2.5cm (1in) piece fresh ginger, peeled and thinly sliced
2 tbsp tamari or soy sauce
250ml (8fl oz) orange juice
1 tbsp caster sugar

1 To remove the excess moisture from the tofu, you need to press it (see page 102). Cube the tofu and place it in a shallow bowl. Whisk together the tamari, orange juice, and salt. Pour the mixture over the tofu and gently toss to combine. Leave the tofu to marinate for at least 30 minutes and as long as overnight.

2 Preheat the oven to 200°C/Gas 6. Drain the tofu. Sprinkle it with the sesame seeds and toss well to coat all over. Spread the canola oil on a baking tray. Scatter the tofu cubes onto the tray in a single layer. Roast for about 15 minutes until golden.

3 Meanwhile, separate the broccoli florets; peel the stalks and slice into discs. To cook the broccoli, heat the oil in a sauté pan over a high heat. Add the ginger and cook for 30 seconds. Stir in the broccoli discs and cook for 2 minutes, stirring often. Add the broccoli florets and cook for a further 1 minute.

4 Add the tamari, orange juice, and sugar. Cover the pan and cook the broccoli, stirring occasionally, for about 5 minutes until tender. Divide the broccoli and tofu among 4 plates and serve immediately.

RECIPE NOTE
• To add more fibre and some unrefined carbohydrates for energy, accompany this dish with steamed brown rice.

garlicky sausage and chard sandwiches

rich in: ✓folate ✓protein

These delicious sandwiches will satisfy your second trimester cravings for bold tastes. Delight your altered palate with the contrasting flavours of rich pork sausage, garlic, and Swiss chard leaves. The sandwiches are hearty, yet not overly filling.

Preparation 10 minutes
Cooking 20 minutes
Makes 2 servings

1 tbsp olive oil

175g (6oz) well-flavoured pork or turkey sausages, removed from skins and crumbled

2 garlic cloves, thinly sliced

1 large bunch Swiss chard, about 550g (1¼lb), stalks discarded and leaves coarsely chopped

¼ tsp sea salt

freshly ground black pepper to taste

1 baguette, 20–25cm (8–10in) long

1 Heat the olive oil in a wide pan over a high heat. Add the sausagemeat and cook, stirring occasionally, for about 3 minutes until browned and crumbly. Using a slotted spoon, transfer the sausagemeat to a plate.
2 Reduce the heat to low and, if necessary, add a bit more olive oil to the pan. Add the garlic and cook for 30 seconds, stirring constantly. Raise the heat to high and add the chard. Season it with the salt and cook for 2 minutes, stirring often.
3 Return the sausagemeat to the pan and add 5 tablespoons water. Stir to mix. Cover the pan and braise, stirring occasionally, for about 3 minutes until the chard is tender. Season with black pepper.
4 Meanwhile, cut the baguette across in half and slice open each half lengthways. To serve, divide the sausage and chard mixture between the baguette halves. Press the halves back together and serve at once.

RECIPE NOTE
• Spinach or sprouting broccoli can be substituted for the chard. Spinach is done as soon as it wilts; sprouting broccoli will need about half the cooking time of the chard, about 5 minutes in total.

wholemeal wraps with tangy white beans and vegetables

rich in: ✓ fibre ✓ carbohydrates

These delicious wraps are a fibre powerhouse, from the wholemeal tortillas, beans, and vegetables. A light fibre-rich meal like this is a great way to keep your bowels moving in the third trimester and post partum, yet won't make you uncomfortably full.

Preparation 10 minutes
Cooking none
Makes 4 servings

1 can (about 425g) white beans, such as haricot or cannellini, drained and rinsed

juice of 1 lemon

2 tbsp roughly chopped almonds

30g (1oz) fresh coriander leaves

½ tsp sea salt

freshly ground black pepper to taste

4 wholemeal flour tortillas or other thin flatbreads, 25cm (10in) in diameter

1 large carrot, scraped and grated

¼ large cucumber, sliced

1 large tomato, thinly sliced

1 roasted red pepper packed in oil, drained and cut into strips

4 romaine or cos lettuce leaves

1 Place the beans, lemon juice, almonds, coriander, and salt in a food processor fitted with the metal blade. Purée the ingredients until smooth. Transfer to a bowl and season with black pepper.

2 To assemble the wraps, spread out the tortillas on a counter. Spoon 2 heaped tablespoons of the white bean mixture onto the centre of each tortilla and spread it out evenly. Add grated carrot, cucumber and tomato slices, strips of red pepper, and a lettuce leaf to each tortilla.

3 Fold in the sides of a tortilla and, from the end nearest you, roll up into a cigar shape. Repeat to roll up the remaining tortillas. Serve at once.

RECIPE NOTES

• Canned black beans can be substituted for the white beans.

• The bean mixture can be prepared several days in advance and kept, tightly covered, in the refrigerator.

• The bean mixture also makes a wonderful dip for raw or lightly steamed vegetables.

baguette pizza

rich in: ✓ **carbohydrates** ✓ **calcium**

Keep some baguettes frozen, and you can quickly fix this delicious pizza when you arrive home from work, tired at the end of a long day – the carbohydrates will re-energize you. The cheese supplies calcium, which you particularly need in the third trimester. That's when most calcium is transported to the baby and the baby's skeleton gets mineralized.

Preparation 10 minutes
Cooking 12 minutes
Makes 4 servings

1 baguette, about 30cm (12in) long

2 cans (about 400g each) whole plum tomatoes in juice, well drained and puréed

1 tbsp caster sugar

½ tsp sea salt

25g (scant 1oz) fresh basil leaves, snipped

4 tbsp grated pecorino cheese

225g (8oz) half-fat mozzarella cheese, sliced or grated

dried oregano to taste

1 Preheat the oven to 200°C/Gas 6. Cut the baguette across in half, then slice each half open lengthways. Place the baguette portions, cut side up, on a baking tray.
2 To prepare the sauce, stir together the puréed tomatoes, sugar, salt, and basil. Spread a thin layer of sauce over the cut surfaces of the baguette portions. Scatter the pecorino and mozzarella evenly over the sauce. Sprinkle with oregano.
3 Place the baking tray in the oven and bake the pizzas for about 12 minutes until the cheese is bubbly. Divide the pizzas among 4 plates and serve hot, with a simple green leaf salad, if you like.

RECIPE NOTES
• Simple toppings, such as blanched broccoli florets and baby leaf spinach, are a great way to add fibre, calcium, and folate to a pizza.
• If you need to add calories to your diet, use regular mozzarella.
• The sauce can also be tossed with freshly cooked pasta.
• When tomatoes are in season and full of flavour, substitute skinned, deseeded, and chopped fresh tomatoes for the canned.

swiss chard and feta frittata

rich in: ✓ **folate** ✓ **omega-3 fatty acids**

A frittata is an Italian-style flat omelette, ideal for a light lunch, quick dinner, or brunch. All leafy green vegetables are rich in folate, and Swiss chard is a particular favourite as it is sweet and earthy, not bitter. Try to use eggs that are enriched with omega-3 fatty acids, to enhance brain and neural development in your baby.

Preparation 10 minutes
Cooking 15 minutes
Makes 2 servings

2 tbsp olive oil

3 garlic cloves, thinly sliced

350g (12oz) green or red Swiss chard, coarsely chopped

½ tsp sea salt

4 eggs

2 egg whites

freshly ground black pepper to taste

60g (2oz) pasteurized feta cheese, crumbled

1 Preheat the oven to 200°C/Gas 6. Heat 1 tablespoon of the olive oil in a 25cm (10in) ovenproof frying pan over a medium heat. Add the garlic and cook for about 45 seconds until soft and fragrant. Add the chard and sprinkle it with the salt. Cover the pan and cook the chard, stirring often, for about 6 minutes until tender.
2 Meanwhile, beat together the eggs and egg whites. Season with black pepper.
3 Drizzle the remaining tablespoon of olive oil into the pan, then add the eggs. After about 1 minute, as the eggs begin to set, push and lift the edges of the frittata with a palette knife and tilt the pan to allow the uncooked egg to run onto the hot pan. Continue cooking the frittata like this for about 3 minutes until the surface is no longer runny but is still wet.
4 Scatter the crumbled cheese evenly over the frittata. Transfer the pan to the oven and cook for about 3 minutes until the cheese softens slightly and the surface of the frittata looks dry. Slide the frittata onto a plate and slice it into wedges. Serve it hot or at room temperature.

RECIPE NOTES
• Spinach can be substituted for the chard. Cook spinach only until it wilts, about 2 minutes over a medium heat.
• If you prefer, you can cook the top of the frittata under a preheated hot grill rather than in the oven.
• For a complete meal, serve the frittata with country bread and a green salad.

steamed broccoli with a divine dipping sauce

rich in: ✓calcium ✓folate ✓fibre

Broccoli is a pregnancy superfood. It is rich in calcium, folate, and fibre; it is simple and quick to prepare; and it is terrific either as a side dish or, as here, a snack. You'll love it with this simple creamy herb dressing, to use as a dipping sauce.

Preparation 10 minutes
Cooking 10 minutes
Makes 4 servings

1kg (2¼lb) broccoli
1 tsp sea salt

Dipping sauce

2 tbsp reduced-fat mayonnaise
2 tbsp Greek yogurt
1 small garlic clove, finely chopped
1 tbsp cider vinegar
1 tbsp caster sugar
½ tsp sea salt
175ml (6fl oz) buttermilk
25g (scant 1oz) fresh flat-leaf parsley leaves, chopped
25g (scant 1oz) fresh coriander leaves, chopped
freshly ground black pepper to taste

1 To prepare the dipping sauce, whisk together the mayonnaise, yogurt, garlic, vinegar, sugar, and salt. Slowly whisk in the buttermilk. Stir in the parsley and coriander. Season the sauce with pepper. Transfer to a serving bowl and set aside.
2 Separate the broccoli florets. Trim and peel the stalks, then cut them into sticks. To steam the broccoli, bring 5cm (2in) of water to the boil in a large saucepan. Add the salt. Stir in the broccoli sticks, cover, and steam for 3 minutes. Add the broccoli florets and stir well, then cover again and steam for a further 3 minutes. Stir the broccoli, then steam, covered, for about 2 more minutes until tender.
3 Drain the broccoli in a colander. Run cold water over the broccoli until it is cool. Transfer to a large platter and serve with the dipping sauce.

RECIPE NOTES
• Both the dipping sauce and broccoli can be prepared a day in advance. Keep, covered, in the refrigerator.
• The dipping sauce also makes a tasty salad dressing and is wonderful with steamed carrots and asparagus, raw mushrooms, and red peppers.

sweet potato and pecan bread

rich in: ✓ protein ✓ fibre

This moist, slightly sweet bread is ideal for a mid-afternoon snack or for breakfast, toasted and spread with a light soft cheese. The tofu and pecans increase the nutritional value by adding protein and fibre, as well as a nice texture. The bread freezes well (up to 2 weeks), so slice it and keep it in your freezer so you can toast one piece at a time.

Preparation 1 hour
Cooking 45–60 minutes
Makes 12 servings

canola (rapeseed) oil or cooking spray for the tin

400g (14oz) mashed sweet potatoes (about 3 medium)

85g (3oz) silken tofu, puréed or thoroughly mashed

150g (5½oz) dark soft brown sugar

2 tbsp clear honey

2 tbsp canola (rapeseed) oil

1 tsp pure vanilla extract

2 eggs

175g (6oz) plain flour

85g (3oz) bread flour

1½ tsp bicarbonate of soda

1 tsp baking powder

1 tsp ground cinnamon

85g (3oz) pecan nuts, coarsely chopped

1 Preheat the oven to 180°C/Gas 4. Lightly coat a 900g (2lb) loaf tin with canola oil or cooking spray and line the bottom with baking parchment.

2 Combine the mashed sweet potatoes, tofu, brown sugar, honey, canola oil, vanilla extract, and eggs in a mixing bowl, stirring well. In another bowl whisk together the flour, bicarbonate of soda, baking powder, and cinnamon. Add to the sweet potato mixture, stirring only enough to combine the ingredients. Gently fold in the pecans.

3 Transfer the mixture to the prepared loaf tin. Place in the oven and bake for 45–60 minutes until a skewer inserted into the centre of the loaf comes out clean. Transfer the bread to a wire rack and allow to cool before slicing.

RECIPE NOTE
• To reduce the preparation time, you can bake the sweet potatoes a day in advance, then peel and mash them when you are ready to make the bread.

tip *Instead of sugary confectionery, fill your cravings for sweets in delicious yet sensible ways, such as with this home-baked tea bread.*

snack bars

rich in: ✓omega-3 fatty acids ✓fibre

Make these fibre-rich, deliciously chewy bars ahead of time and store in the refrigerator, so you can enjoy one as a snack any time. Each bar also makes a complete breakfast in itself. Linseed (flax seed) is one of the few vegetarian sources of omega-3 fatty acids, which are important in foetal brain development, especially in the third trimester.

Preparation 15 minutes
Cooking 18 minutes
Makes 9 bars

canola (rapeseed) oil or cooking spray for the tin

115g (4oz) linseed (flax seed)

120ml (4fl oz) apple juice concentrate

150ml (5fl oz) brown rice syrup

2 tbsp maple syrup

8 dates, pitted and chopped

75g (2½oz) sultanas

175g (6oz) rolled oats

30g (1oz) crisp-rice cereal

1 tsp baking powder

4 tbsp sunflower seeds

4 tbsp toasted wheat germ

1 Preheat the oven to 180°C/Gas 4. Lightly grease a 23cm (9in) square baking tin with canola oil or cooking spray. Grind the linseed in a clean coffee grinder until it resembles flour. Set it aside.

2 Combine the apple juice concentrate, brown rice syrup, and maple syrup in a small saucepan. Gently heat the mixture until it is warm. Set it aside.

3 Place the dates and sultanas in a food processor fitted with the metal blade and process until the fruit is puréed and clumps into a ball. Transfer the fruit purée to a mixing bowl.

4 Place the rolled oats, rice cereal, and baking powder in the food processor and process for 10 seconds. Transfer to the mixing bowl containing the fruit purée. Add the ground linseed, sunflower seeds, and wheat germ to the bowl. Combine the ingredients thoroughly. Pour the juice and syrup mixture into the mixing bowl and knead the ingredients together until they are well combined.

5 Spread the mixture evenly in the prepared tin. Bake for about 18 minutes until a skewer inserted into the centre comes out clean. Remove from the oven and leave to cool slightly, then cut into 9 bars. When they are completely cold, remove from the tin and wrap individually in cling film. Keep in the refrigerator for up to 3 days.

RECIPE NOTES
• Sliced dried figs can be substituted for the dates.
• If you don't have a coffee grinder, you can put the linseed in a deep bowl and grind with a hand blender. Cover the top of the bowl to prevent the seeds flying out. This will not produce as fine a result as when using a coffee grinder, but the linseed will be sufficiently ground for the recipe.

chocolate and dried cherry scones

rich in: ✓antioxidants ✓fibre

Craving chocolate? Who doesn't! Dark chocolate is a rich source of antioxidants, and studies show that mums who eat chocolate during pregnancy have babies who exhibit more smiling behaviour at six months of age. These scones freeze well, so make a batch at the weekend. Then you can reheat one quickly to enjoy with a cup of tea.

Preparation 10 minutes
Cooking 12 minutes
Makes 8 scones

canola (rapeseed) oil or cooking spray for the baking tray
210g (7½oz) plain white flour
60g (2oz) wholemeal flour
1 tbsp baking powder
¼ tsp sea salt
65g (2¼oz) caster sugar
60g (2oz) cold unsalted butter
1 egg, at room temperature
5–6 tbsp whole milk, or more if needed
75g (2½oz) dried cherries
85g (3oz) good dark chocolate, cut into small chunks

1 Preheat the oven to 190°C/Gas 5. Lightly grease or spray a baking tray. Set aside.
2 In a large bowl, combine the plain flour, wholemeal flour, baking powder, salt, and sugar. Mix the ingredients together well. With your fingertips, rub the butter into the dry ingredients until the mixture is crumbly.
3 In a medium bowl, whisk together the eggs and milk. Stir into the dry ingredients, mixing only enough to moisten them. The dough will be sticky. Fold in the dried cherries and chocolate chunks.
4 Turn the dough out onto a lightly floured surface and flatten into a circle that is 2cm (¾in) thick. Cut the dough circle into 8 wedge-shaped scones. Arrange the scones 1cm (½in) apart on the prepared baking tray.
5 Bake the scones for about 12 minutes until they are light golden brown and cooked through. Transfer to a wire rack to cool. Serve warm or at room temperature.

RECIPE NOTES

• Once cold, the scones can be frozen: wrap individually in foil, then pack in a freezer bag. They can be kept in the freezer for up to 6 months. To reheat from frozen, remove from the bag and put the foil-wrapped scones on a baking tray. Reheat in a preheated 180°C/Gas 4 oven for about 10 minutes until thawed and heated through. Leave to cool for 1–2 minutes before serving.
• For those trying to minimize weight gain, use skimmed milk in place of whole milk. For a higher calorie version, for those trying to gain weight, use single cream.
• Dried cranberries or dried blueberries, both rich sources of antioxidants, can be substituted for the dried cherries.

soups, salads, and sides

There are few meals more satisfying and nutritious on a cool evening than a steaming bowl of soup. You don't have to use elaborate ingredients, as everything you need is probably already on hand in your kitchen. Salads can be a main course or an accompaniment to a soup or light meal. The varieties of salads you can make are endless, so be creative. Side dishes are a good way to add the extra nutrients you need in pregnancy, as well as to complement a main dish.

Most soups are quick to prepare, with the majority of the cooking time unattended, just a stir now and then. If you are facing a busy week, prepare for it by making a hearty soup at the weekend. Then you can just reheat it when you want to eat. A soup that contains beans, meat, or tofu, grains, and a variety of vegetables is a one-pot meal that provides all the nutrients you and your baby need.

A salad doesn't have to be just one kind of lettuce topped with tomatoes and cucumbers. Use a mixture of lettuces and other greens and top with toasted nuts, cheeses, or cooked beans as a protein source. Add dried cranberries, cherries, and raisins for sweet flavours, or sliced fresh fruits like mangoes and apples, and sprinkle with toasted sesame seeds. The best salads are those that make use of produce at its ripest and freshest. Add spark to your vinaigrette dressing by using different vinegars. Vary the oils too – olive to walnut to groundnut, all of which offer heart-healthy fats.

Try some dark green, leafy vegetables as side dishes. Leafy greens are a food to use in abundance, since they tend to be high in iron, calcium, and folate, which are three of the most important nutrients in pregnancy. The bold taste of greens will appeal to your pregnant palate. Another great side dish is mashed potatoes. When you're nauseous in the first trimester, you might even want to try them for breakfast.

spicy lentil and cauliflower soup

rich in: ✓ fibre ✓ iron

With plenty of fibre and iron, lentils are very nutritious. This lentil soup freezes very well, so plan ahead and prepare a batch while you are still pregnant. Then have your partner bring it to you after you have had your baby, for a delightful and easily digested post-partum meal. You can also enjoy it any time your bowels are sluggish.

Preparation 15 minutes
Cooking 1 hour
Makes 4 servings

1 tbsp olive oil

175g (6oz) spicy or well-flavoured sausages, removed from skins and crumbled

2 garlic cloves, sliced

1 onion, diced

1 tsp sea salt

2 carrots, scraped and diced

2 celery sticks, diced

225g (8oz) red lentils

½ cauliflower, cut into 1cm (½in) pieces

50g (1¾oz) fresh flat-leaf parsley, chopped

1 Heat the olive oil in a large saucepan over a high heat. Add the sausagemeat and brown it for 2 minutes, stirring often. Using a slotted spoon, transfer the sausage to a plate and set aside.

2 Reduce the heat to low. Add the garlic to the pan and cook for 30 seconds. Add the onion and sprinkle it with the salt. Cook, stirring often, for about 2 minutes until the onion is soft. Raise the heat slightly and add the carrots and celery. Cook for a further 3 minutes, stirring often.

3 Raise the heat to high and add the lentils and 1 litre (1¾ pints) water. Return the sausage to the pan. Bring the soup to the boil, then reduce the heat and simmer for 40 minutes, stirring occasionally. Add the cauliflower and continue simmering for about 10 minutes until the lentils are tender.

4 To serve, divide the soup among 4 bowls, garnish each portion with a sprinkling of parsley, and serve at once.

RECIPE NOTE

• The soup can be prepared several days in advance. When reheating, add a bit of water if the soup is too thick.

beef, barley, and escarole soup

rich in: ✓ iron ✓ vitamin C

This delicious soup follows the principle that iron (here from beef) is best absorbed when combined with vitamin C (here from tomatoes). It is also rich in fibre from the barley and folate from the escarole. The soup takes time to cook, but you don't have to pay much attention to it while it simmers away, filling your house with wonderful aromas.

Preparation 15 minutes
Cooking 1½ hours
Makes 4 servings

1 tbsp olive oil

675g (1½lb) boneless beef chuck or brisket, trimmed of all visible fat and then cubed

2 tsp sea salt

2 garlic cloves, thinly sliced

1 onion, diced

2 carrots, scraped and diced

2 celery sticks, diced

100g (3½oz) pearl barley

2 litres (3½ pints) unsalted beef or chicken stock

1 can (about 400g) chopped tomatoes in juice

350g (12oz) escarole, chopped

freshly ground black pepper to taste

1 Heat the olive oil in a large saucepan over a high heat. Meanwhile, sprinkle the beef with 1 teaspoon of the salt. When the oil is hot, carefully (watch for splattering) place the cubes of beef in the pan. Sauté the beef, stirring occasionally, for about 7 minutes until well browned all over. Using tongs or a slotted spoon, transfer the beef cubes to a plate and set aside.

2 Reduce the heat to medium and add the garlic to the pan. Cook for 1 minute. Add the onion and sprinkle it with the remaining salt. Cook for 2 minutes. Add the carrots and celery, and cook for a further 2 minutes, stirring often.

3 Return the beef to the pan. Raise the heat slightly, cover the pan, and sweat the ingredients for 3 minutes. Raise the heat to high and add the barley, stock, and tomatoes with their juice. Cover the pan again and bring the soup to the boil. Reduce the heat and simmer for about 1¼ hours until the beef is tender.

4 Stir in the escarole. It will begin to wilt immediately. Season the soup with black pepper and, if necessary, more salt. Divide the soup among 4 large bowls and serve.

RECIPE NOTE

• Spinach or Swiss chard can be substituted for the escarole, which is a type of endive. They are both rich in folate. Like escarole, spinach will wilt immediately, whereas Swiss chard will need to simmer for about 7 minutes to become tender.

sesame chicken salad

rich in: ✓**protein** ✓**folate**

When you are in your third trimester, you may feel hot much of the time, because your metabolism has speeded up. Something cool may be your preference, but not a salad of raw ingredients. This warm salad will be ideal. Most chicken salads are laden with mayonnaise, but this heart-healthy version uses a canola (rapeseed) oil dressing.

Preparation 10 minutes
Cooking 25 minutes
Makes 4 servings

30g (1oz) slivered almonds
350g (12oz) skinless, boneless chicken breast, cut into strips
½ tsp sea salt
60g (2oz) sesame seeds
3 tbsp canola (rapeseed) oil
4 tbsp orange juice
2 tsp Dijon mustard
2 tbsp clear honey
1 large romaine or cos lettuce, chopped
1 cucumber, sliced
1 carrot, scraped and grated

1 Preheat the oven to 200°C/Gas 6. Place the almonds in a small frying pan over a low heat. Toast them, shaking the pan occasionally, for 10 minutes until golden.
2 Meanwhile, place the chicken strips in a bowl. Sprinkle with the salt and sesame seeds, and toss well, being certain the sesame seeds adhere to the chicken. Drizzle 1 tablespoon of the oil onto a small baking tray. Place the chicken on the tray, turning to coat each piece with oil. Spread out the chicken in a single layer. Place in the oven and bake the chicken for about 18 minutes until golden and cooked through.
3 While the chicken is cooking, prepare the dressing by whisking together the remaining 2 tablespoons of oil, the orange juice, mustard, and honey.
4 To assemble the salads, divide the chopped lettuce among 4 large bowls and garnish each portion with cucumber slices, grated carrot, and toasted almonds. Spoon 2–3 tablespoons of dressing over each salad and toss well. Top each salad with strips of chicken and serve immediately.

RECIPE NOTES
• The chicken can be prepared several hours in advance. When it has cooled, refrigerate it until serving time.
• A combination of lettuces and salad greens can be substituted for the romaine or cos. Red and green leaf lettuces, iceberg lettuce, spinach, and mesclun (baby salad greens) are all excellent choices.

black bean and bulghur salad with parsley and lemon

rich in: ✓ fibre ✓ carbohydrates

This salad is packed with a double dose of fibre, so have it as a side dish or snack when the hormone progesterone slows the bowels and causes constipation. Both bulgur wheat and black beans are nutritional powerhouses, and make great pregnancy storecupboard foods.

Preparation 30 minutes
Cooking none
Chilling 1 hour
Makes 4 servings

150g (5½oz) bulghur wheat

¾ tsp sea salt

1 can (about 425g) black beans, drained and well rinsed

50g (1¾oz) fresh flat-leaf parsley leaves, chopped

4 spring onions, thinly sliced

350g (12oz) cherry tomatoes, halved

1 tbsp olive oil

juice of 1 lemon

freshly ground black pepper to taste

1 Bring 500ml (17fl oz) water to the boil in a saucepan. Stir in the bulghur wheat and ½ teaspoon of the salt. Return the water to the boil, then remove from the heat and cover the pan. Leave the bulghur to soak for about 20 minutes until the water has been absorbed.
2 Meanwhile, combine the black beans, parsley, spring onions, and cherry tomatoes in a large bowl.
3 Add the soaked bulghur to the bowl. Stir in the olive oil, lemon juice, and remaining salt. Season the salad with black pepper. Cover the bowl and chill the salad for at least 1 hour before serving.

RECIPE NOTES
• As with many salads, the flavour intensifies with time, so consider preparing this 2 or 3 days in advance and keep it refrigerated.
• If you need to increase your calorie consumption, drizzle olive oil over your salad.

tip *Bulghur is a wheat product made by steaming and drying wheat kernels, and then cracking them. Because it is minimally processed, its nutritional value is similar to whole wheat.*

romaine salad with mint, dates, oranges, and almonds

rich in: ✓ folate ✓ calcium

This is a perfect pregnancy salad, as it will simultaneously satisfy your cravings for salt and sweets. It is a great combination of contrasting tastes and textures: salty (capers) and sweet (dates and orange); crunchy (almonds) and soft (dates).

Preparation 10 minutes
Cooking 10 minutes
Makes 4 servings

30g (1oz) flaked almonds

½ tsp sea salt

1 large romaine or cos lettuce, chopped

8 Medjool dates, pitted and sliced

1 large navel orange, peeled and cut into 1cm (½in) slices

2 tbsp capers, rinsed

juice of 1 lemon

2 tbsp olive oil

1 tsp caster sugar

6 fresh mint leaves, thinly sliced

1 Place the flaked almonds in a small frying pan over a low heat and sprinkle them with the salt. Toast them, shaking the pan occasionally, for about 10 minutes until they are golden brown.
2 Meanwhile, combine the lettuce, dates, orange slices, and capers in a large salad bowl. Set aside.
3 To prepare the dressing, whisk together the lemon juice, olive oil, sugar, and mint.
4 Pour the dressing over the salad and toss well. Divide the salad among 4 large plates. Garnish each with a tablespoon of toasted almonds and serve at once.

RECIPE NOTE
• This salad makes a great side dish or, with some crusty bread, a light lunch. It is an ideal accompaniment to Simply Quick Pan-Fried Steak (page 155).

tip *Try this salad when your hormones are high and the heat is getting to you. It is sure to have a calming, cooling effect, and won't leave you feeling overly full.*

cucumbers with onion, mint, and feta

rich in: ✓ calcium ✓ vitamin C

Cool cucumbers are paired with zesty red onions and tangy mint in this light and refreshing salad. It combines lots of flavours and textures, and the feta will satisfy your craving for salt. Enjoy this on a hot day – you'll find it cools and soothes. Your baby generates heat inside you, which is why pregnant women are often hotter than other women!

Preparation 10 minutes
Cooking none
Chilling 1 hour
Makes 4 servings

2 cucumbers
1 red onion, thinly sliced
6 fresh mint leaves, thinly sliced
2 tbsp olive oil
¼ tsp sea salt
freshly ground black pepper to taste
115g (4oz) pasteurized feta cheese, crumbled

1 Cut each cucumber in half lengthways, then cut across into 2.5cm (1in) pieces.
2 Combine the cucumbers, red onion, mint, olive oil, and salt in a large serving bowl. Toss well together. Season the salad with black pepper.
3 Garnish the salad with the crumbled feta. Cover the bowl and chill for at least 1 hour before serving.

RECIPE NOTE
• Accompany the salad with crusty bread for a light lunch.

tip *Be sure to read the label on the feta cheese before you buy it, to check that it is made from pasteurized milk.*

chilled pasta with broccoli, spinach, and tomatoes in a creamy dressing

rich in: ✓ protein ✓ calcium ✓ folate

This pasta salad tastes even better the second day, so make it ahead of time for better flavour as well as convenience. The creamy dressing is not based on mayonnaise, but on silken tofu, which is rich in protein and calcium. The broccoli adds some folate and fibre.

Preparation 10 minutes
Cooking 10 minutes
Chilling 1 hour
Makes 4 servings

100g (3½oz) dry-pack sun-dried tomatoes

115g (4oz) baby spinach leaves

225g (8oz) macaroni or other short pasta shapes

675g (1½lb) broccoli, cut into bite-sized florets

Dressing

2 tbsp balsamic vinegar

½ tsp sea salt

115g (4oz) silken tofu

50g (1¾oz) Parmesan or pecorino cheese, freshly grated

freshly ground black pepper to taste

1 Place the tomatoes in a bowl. Pour boiling water over them and leave them to soak for about 10 minutes until softened. Drain them and thinly slice.

2 While the tomatoes are soaking, place the spinach in a colander in the sink. Bring a large pan of salted water to the boil. Stir in the pasta and cook for 4 minutes. Stir the broccoli into the boiling pasta water and cook the pasta and broccoli together for 2–3 minutes until the pasta is *al dente* and the broccoli is bright green and just tender. Drain the pasta and broccoli in the colander containing the spinach. Run cold water over the pasta and vegetables to stop their cooking. When all the ingredients are cooled and drained, transfer to a large bowl. Add the tomatoes. Set aside.

3 To prepare the dressing, combine the vinegar, salt, and tofu in a blender or food processor fitted with the metal blade. Process until smooth. Stir in the cheese and season with black pepper.

4 Pour the dressing over the pasta and vegetables, and toss well. Cover the bowl and chill the salad for at least an hour before serving.

RECIPE NOTE

• Fresh lemon juice or raspberry, herb, or red wine vinegar can be substituted for the balsamic vinegar.

couscous with olive oil and flat-leaf parsley

rich in: ✓ carbohydrates

Make this in the first trimester when you are most likely to be nauseous, and eat it as a main course – you'll find it very soothing and satisfying. Later during your pregnancy, and post partum, serve it as an accompaniment for meat, poultry, fish, or vegetables.

Preparation 5 minutes
Cooking 15 minutes
Makes 4 servings

500ml (17fl oz) lightly salted chicken stock or water

3 tbsp best-quality olive oil

½ tsp sea salt

175g (6oz) couscous

25g (scant 1oz) fresh flat-leaf parsley leaves, chopped

1 Pour the chicken stock or water into a medium-sized saucepan and bring to the boil. Add the olive oil and salt, then stir in the couscous. Remove the pan from the heat and cover it tightly. Leave the couscous to steam for about 10 minutes until all of the stock or water has been absorbed.

2 With a fork, fluff up and separate the couscous grains, then stir in the chopped parsley. Serve at once.

RECIPE NOTE
• Fresh coriander or basil can be substituted for the parsley.

tip *Although it looks like a grain, couscous is in fact a type of pasta. It is rich in carbohydrate, which means a dish like this will energize you.*

mashed potatoes with olive oil and fried garlic

rich in: ✓**carbohydrate**

Mashed potatoes are a true comfort food, and if you are craving strong tastes, you'll love this version, which is perfumed with golden-fried garlic. Instead of lots of butter, it is made with heart-healthy olive oil. This side dish is great with Salty Tuscan Pork Chops (page 157).

Preparation 10 minutes
Cooking 30–40 minutes
Makes 4 servings

900g (2lb) large floury potatoes, scrubbed

15g (½oz) unsalted butter

2 tbsp olive oil

6 garlic cloves, thinly sliced

½ tsp sea salt

freshly ground black pepper to taste

about 175ml (6fl oz) milk, warmed

1 Place the unpeeled potatoes in a large saucepan. Add water to cover them by 2.5cm (1in). Bring the water to the boil, then reduce the heat and simmer the potatoes for about 30 minutes until they are tender.

2 While the potatoes are cooking, combine the butter and olive oil in a frying pan over a medium heat. When the mixture stops sizzling, add the garlic. Reduce the heat slightly and fry the garlic, stirring occasionally, for about 7 minutes until golden. Remove from the heat.

3 Drain the potatoes. When they are cool enough to handle, carefully peel off the skin, then cut the potatoes into big chunks. Place the chunks in the still warm saucepan. Mash the potatoes with a potato masher. Add the salt, black pepper, and garlic mixture, then gradually mash in enough warm milk to achieve the consistency you like. Serve immediately.

RECIPE NOTE
• If you're feeling very nauseous, try this recipe without the garlic.

tip *New evidence suggests that fat type, not total content, is what is important in a heart-healthy diet – heart risk can start in utero. Get into good habits by using olive oil for all your cooking.*

roasted asparagus with pine nuts and blue cheese

rich in: ✓folates ✓fibre

Roasting asparagus brings out its natural sweetness and concentrates its flavour, and this folate-rich recipe has plenty of assertive tastes and contrasting textures. You need folate in increased amounts throughout your pregnancy, and asparagus is one of the richest sources.

Preparation 5 minutes
Cooking 20 minutes
Makes 4 servings

35g (1¼oz) pine nuts
675g (1½lb) asparagus
½ tsp sea salt
1 tbsp olive oil
60g (2oz) pasteurized
Gorgonzola cheese, crumbled

1 Preheat the oven to 200°C/Gas 6. Place the pine nuts in a small frying pan over a low heat. Toast them, shaking the pan occasionally, for about 5 minutes until golden and fragrant. Transfer to kitchen paper.

2 Place the asparagus spears in one layer on a baking tray. Sprinkle them with the salt, drizzle with the olive oil, and toss well. Roast the asparagus for 8–12 minutes until tender and lightly charred.

3 Transfer the asparagus to a serving platter. Dot with the Gorgonzola cheese, sprinkle with the pine nuts, and serve at once.

RECIPE NOTES

• Select asparagus spears that are slightly thicker than pencils.

• Read the label on the Gorgonzola cheese to ensure that it is made with pasteurized milk. Pasteurization will kill the bacterium listeria, allowing for safe consumption during pregnancy. Pregnant women should not eat unpasteurized soft cheeses.

• For a lower calorie and lower fat version, but one that still has plenty of flavour, omit the Gorgonzola cheese and instead squeeze a fresh lemon over the asparagus before sprinkling them with the pine nuts.

braised kale with spicy sausage

rich in: ✓**antioxidants** ✓**fibre** ✓**folate**

Dark leafy greens such as kale, spring greens, spinach, and Swiss chard are real stars, since they offer many important nutrients for a healthy pregnancy: great amounts of antioxidants, fibre, calcium, and folate. In addition, they are simple to prepare and adapt well to many different flavourings. Here, spicy sausage gives zing to the greens.

Preparation 10 minutes
Cooking 45 minutes
Makes 4 servings

1 tbsp olive oil

175g (6oz) spicy pork sausages, removed from skins and crumbled

1 onion, diced

½ tsp sea salt

450g (1lb) kale, coarsely chopped

350ml (12fl oz) lightly salted chicken stock or water

1 Heat the olive oil in a large saucepan over a high heat. Add the sausagemeat and brown it for 3 minutes, stirring often.

2 Add the onion and sprinkle it with the salt. Cook for about 1 minute until the onion begins to soften, stirring often.

3 Add the kale to the pan and cook, stirring constantly, for about 2 minutes until the kale begins to wilt.

4 Stir in the stock or water and bring to the boil. Reduce the heat and cover the pan. Braise the kale for about 40 minutes until it is tender, stirring occasionally.

5 Transfer the kale to a shallow bowl and serve hot or at room temperature.

tip *Dark green leafy vegetables are pregnancy superfoods. Their strong tastes will appeal to the altered pregnancy palate and they are also nutritional powerhouses.*

cinnamon-scented butternut squash

rich in: ✓ **antioxidants** ✓ **fibre**

Caramelizing is a process that brings out the natural sweetness in foods, and is a healthful way to satisfy your craving for sweets. This roasted caramelized squash makes an interesting and colourful garnish for pasta tossed with wilted greens (spinach, spring greens, and Swiss chard are all good choices).

Preparation 10 minutes
Cooking 45 minutes
Makes 4 servings

1 large butternut squash, about 900g (2lb)

¾ tsp ground cinnamon

good pinch of grated nutmeg

2 tbsp canola (rapeseed) oil

½ tsp sea salt

55g (scant 2oz) dark soft brown sugar

1 Preheat the oven to 220°C/Gas 7. Peel and seed the squash, then cut into 5cm (2in) pieces. Place in a large bowl and add the cinnamon, nutmeg, oil, salt, and brown sugar. Toss to mix well and coat all the pieces of squash.

2 Transfer the squash to a heavy baking tray and spread out the pieces in a single layer. Roast the squash for 45 minutes until it is very tender and caramelized. If necessary, turn the baking tray and stir the squash halfway through cooking to be sure it cooks evenly. Serve hot.

RECIPE NOTE

• Don't worry if the corners of the squash pieces look charred. They will be incredibly sweet and tender.

tip *Vegetables with deep orange flesh, such as butternut squash, sweet potatoes, and carrots, contain the greatest amounts of beta-carotene.*

roasted provençal vegetables

rich in: ✓ folate ✓ fibre

In this recipe, vegetables are roasted with nothing more than salt, black pepper, and olive oil, so that their individual flavours and textures are retained. Since there is no one vegetable that will provide you with all the vitamins and nutrients you need in pregnancy, the key to good nutrition is to consume a variety of vegetables, as in this dish.

Preparation 10 minutes
Cooking 40 minutes
Makes 4 servings

1 medium red pepper, cored

1 medium green pepper, cored

2 aubergines, halved lengthways

2 courgettes, halved lengthways

1 medium red onion

8 garlic cloves, peeled

1 tsp sea salt

2 tbsp olive oil

freshly ground black pepper to taste

1 Preheat the oven to 220°C/Gas 7. Cut the peppers, aubergines, courgettes, and red onion into 5cm (2in) pieces. Transfer them to a large, heavy roasting tin and toss together with the garlic cloves.

2 Sprinkle the vegetables with the salt and drizzle with the olive oil. Season with black pepper. Toss well again, then spread out in a single layer. Place in the oven and roast the vegetables for 20 minutes.

3 Remove the tin from the oven and gently stir the vegetables, keeping them in a single layer. Return the tin to the oven and continue roasting the vegetables for 10–20 minutes until they are soft and slightly caramelized. Serve the vegetables hot or at room temperature.

RECIPE NOTE
• The vegetables are wonderful as an accompaniment to any grilled or roast meat, fish, or poultry. They also can be tossed with pasta or used as a sandwich filling.

steamed couscous with spring vegetables and feta

rich in: ✓ folate ✓ carbohydrates

Couscous is a type of pasta that is light and delicious. It won't leave you feeling full and uncomfortable, and it may soothe a nauseous stomach. Pairing couscous with asparagus, fresh sweetcorn, and tomatoes will give you and your baby a folate punch.

Preparation 20 minutes
Cooking 20 minutes
Makes 4 servings

500g (1lb 2oz) couscous
½ tsp sea salt
115g (4oz) pasteurized feta cheese, crumbled

Vegetables
1 tbsp olive oil
2 garlic cloves, thinly sliced
350g (12oz) asparagus, cut into 5cm (2in) pieces
kernels cut from 2 cobs fresh sweetcorn
½ tsp sea salt
250ml (8fl oz) lightly salted chicken stock
350g (12oz) cherry tomatoes, halved
50g (1¾oz) fresh basil, snipped or torn
freshly ground black pepper to taste

1 To steam the couscous, bring 650ml (22fl oz) water to the boil in a medium-sized saucepan with a tight-fitting lid. Stir in the salt and couscous. Remove from the heat and cover the pan. Leave the couscous to steam for 10–20 minutes until it is tender and all of the water has been absorbed.

2 Meanwhile, to prepare the vegetables, heat the olive oil in a large saucepan over a medium heat. Add the garlic and cook for 45 seconds. Raise the heat to high and add the asparagus. Cook for 2 minutes, stirring often. Add the sweetcorn kernels and salt. Cook for a further 1 minute, stirring often.

3 Pour in the chicken stock and bring to the boil. Simmer for about 2 minutes until the asparagus and sweetcorn are tender. Remove the pan from the heat and stir in the tomatoes and basil. Season with black pepper.

4 Stir the steamed couscous into the vegetables and fluff with a fork. Divide the couscous and vegetables among 4 shallow bowls. Garnish each portion with feta cheese and serve at once.

RECIPE NOTE

• Israeli couscous, which is larger than the Moroccan variety – about the size of a peppercorn – and is toasted, is also delicious in this dish.

white rice with red sauce

rich in: ✓ carbohydrates ✓ vitamin C

This plain and comforting rice dish may be all you can face on difficult days in the first trimester. Most women find bland carbohydrates – rice, pasta, and potatoes – settle their stomachs in the difficult times when nausea abounds. Seared scallops can be added for the rest of the family – and you can enjoy them too, when you are feeling better.

Preparation 10 minutes
Cooking 30 minutes
Makes 4 servings

300g (10oz) long-grain white rice

4 tbsp grated pecorino cheese

Red sauce

1 tbsp olive oil

2 garlic cloves, thinly sliced

1 onion, diced

½ tsp sea salt

2 cans (about 400g each) whole plum tomatoes, puréed with juice

50g (1¾ oz) fresh basil leaves, snipped

freshly ground black pepper to taste

Seared scallops (optional)

1 tbsp olive oil

12 scallops, thoroughly dried

¼ tsp sea salt

8 fresh basil leaves, shredded

1 To prepare the rice, bring 750ml (1¼ pints) water to the boil in a medium-sized saucepan. Stir in the rice. Return the water to the boil, then cover the pan tightly and reduce the heat. Simmer the rice very gently for about 20 minutes until it is tender and all of the water has been absorbed.

2 Meanwhile, make the sauce. Heat the olive oil in a saucepan over a medium heat. Add the garlic and cook for 45 seconds. Add the onion and sprinkle it with the salt. Cook the onion for about 3 minutes until it is soft, stirring occasionally. Raise the heat to high and add the puréed tomatoes. Bring to the boil. Reduce the heat and simmer the sauce for about 20 minutes until thickened, stirring occasionally. Stir in the basil and season the sauce with black pepper.

3 Just before the rice and sauce are ready, cook the scallops, if serving them. Heat the oil in a large sauté pan over a high heat. Season the scallops with the salt and black pepper. When the oil is hot, place the scallops in the pan in a single layer. Sear for about 1½ minutes until golden. Turn them over and sear the other side for about 1 minute, cooking until the scallops are opaque in the middle. Remove from the heat, add the basil, and toss with the scallops.

4 To serve, divide the rice among 4 shallow bowls. Spoon the sauce over the rice and sprinkle with the cheese. Top with the hot scallops.

RECIPE NOTE

• The sauce can be prepared up to 3 days in advance and refrigerated in an airtight container. It can also be frozen for up to 1 month.

spaghetti with asparagus and toasted walnuts

rich in: ✓folate ✓omega-3 fatty acids

This incredibly simple pasta dish is likely to become a favourite in your house. Asparagus is rich in folate, and walnuts are an excellent source of omega-3 fatty acids, to fuel the development of your baby's nervous system. The carbohydrates from the pasta will energize you.

Preparation 10 minutes
Cooking 15–20 minutes
Makes 4 servings

450g (1lb) spaghetti

125g (4½oz) walnuts, coarsely chopped

2 tbsp olive oil

2 garlic cloves, thinly sliced

675g (1½lb) asparagus, sliced diagonally into 5cm (2in) pieces

300ml (10fl oz) lightly salted chicken stock

½ tsp sea salt

freshly ground black pepper to taste

40g (1½oz) Parmesan or pecorino cheese, freshly grated

1 Bring a large saucepan of salted water to the boil. Add the pasta and cook according to the packet instructions.

2 Meanwhile, place the walnuts in a small frying pan over a low heat. Toast them, shaking the pan occasionally, for 5–7 minutes until they are fragrant.

3 While the walnuts are toasting, heat the olive oil in another large saucepan over a medium heat. Add the garlic and cook for 30 seconds. Raise the heat to high and stir in the asparagus. Cook, tossing often, for about 5 minutes until the asparagus is bright green. Add the chicken stock and salt. Cook, stirring occasionally, for about 4 minutes until the asparagus is just tender.

4 Drain the pasta and add it to the sauce. Toss the sauce and pasta together, then simmer for 1 minute, tossing often with tongs. Season the dish with black pepper and more salt, if necessary. Divide the pasta among 4 large plates, garnish with the cheese and toasted walnuts, and serve immediately.

RECIPE NOTE

• An equal amount of broccoli florets can be substituted for the asparagus. In step 3, reduce the cooking time to 3 minutes before adding the chicken stock.

linguine with prawns, tomatoes, and parsley

rich in: ✓ **carbohydrates** ✓ **protein**

Seafood such as prawns, clams, and mussels is safe for consumption in pregnancy, as long as it is cooked. Try this simple yet tasty version of prawns and pasta tossed in a garlicky tomato sauce. If you like, sprinkle with freshly grated Parmesan cheese before serving.

Preparation 10 minutes
Cooking 15–20 minutes
Makes 4 servings

450g (1lb) linguine

1 tbsp olive oil

15g (½oz) unsalted butter

5 garlic cloves, thinly sliced

5 canned plum tomatoes, drained (juice reserved) and coarsely chopped

450g (1lb) raw tiger or king prawns without heads, peeled

30g (1oz) fresh flat-leaf parsley, chopped

1 tsp sea salt

freshly ground black pepper to taste

1 Bring a large saucepan of salted water to the boil. Add the pasta and cook according to the packet instructions.

2 Meanwhile, combine the olive oil and butter in another large saucepan over a medium heat. When the sizzling stops, add the garlic and cook for 2 minutes, taking care not to let it burn. Raise the heat to high and add the tomatoes. Make the reserved tomato juice up to 250ml (8fl oz) and add to the pan. Cook for 2 minutes, stirring occasionally.

3 Add the prawns and parsley, and cook, stirring often, for about 2 minutes until the prawns are pink and firm. Season with the salt and black pepper.

4 Drain the pasta and stir it into the sauce. Reduce the heat to low and cook the pasta and sauce together for 2 minutes, stirring occasionally. Divide the pasta among 4 shallow bowls and serve.

tip *In general, fish and shellfish are lower in fat and cholesterol when compared to beef, poultry, and dairy products.*

seared salmon on wilted mesclun with raspberry vinaigrette

rich in: ✓ omega-3 fatty acids ✓ folate ✓ protein

The foetal brain undergoes growth throughout pregnancy, with the most rapid growth in the third trimester. Studies show that a maternal diet rich in omega-3 fatty acids will enhance brain development. A major source of omega-3 fats is oily fish, such as salmon.

Preparation 10 minutes
Cooking 10 minutes
Makes 4 servings

2 tsp olive oil

675g (1½lb) salmon fillet (preferably cut from the thick end), cut into 4 portions

½ tsp sea salt

freshly ground black pepper to taste

Greens

350g (12oz) mesclun (see right)

2 tbsp olive oil

4 tbsp raspberry vinegar

¼ tsp sea salt

1 Heat the oil in a heavy frying pan over a high heat. Meanwhile, sprinkle the salmon portions on both sides with the salt and some black pepper. When the oil begins to smoke, carefully place the salmon, skin side down, in the pan. Sear the salmon for 5–6 minutes. Carefully flip the pieces over and sear for a further 4–5 minutes until just cooked through. Transfer the salmon to a plate and keep warm.

2 Place the mesclun in a large bowl. Whisk together the olive oil, raspberry vinegar, salt, and black pepper. Pour the dressing over the mesclun and toss well.

3 To serve, remove the skin from each piece of salmon. Divide the dressed mesclun among 4 large dinner plates. Place the salmon on the salad greens and serve at once. The heat from the salmon will slowly wilt the greens.

RECIPE NOTES

• Mesclun is a mix of small, young salad leaves. Baby spinach leaves can be substituted for the mesclun.

• Wild salmon has the highest amounts of omega-3 fatty acids, but farmed salmon is a good alternative.

herb and mustard-crusted salmon

rich in: ✓**omega-3 fatty acids** ✓**protein**

As a heart-healthy protein food that is rich in healthy fats, salmon is a pregnancy superstar. It is wonderful when just seared, but adding a herb crust takes this fish to new culinary heights with little extra effort. The herbs in this recipe are only suggestions – experiment and develop your favourite combination.

Preparation 10 minutes
Cooking 15 minutes
Makes 4 servings

25g (scant 1oz) fresh flat-leaf parsley leaves

25g (scant 1oz) fresh coriander leaves

3 spring onions

3 tsp olive oil

1 tbsp Dijon mustard

juice of ½ lemon

675g (1½lb) salmon fillet (preferably cut from the thick end), skinned

¼ tsp sea salt

freshly ground black pepper to taste

1 Preheat the oven to 230°C/Gas 8. Chop together the parsley, coriander, and spring onions until well combined. In a small bowl, whisk together 2 teaspoons of the olive oil, the mustard, and lemon juice.

2 Sprinkle the salmon on both sides with the salt and some black pepper. Brush the olive oil mixture on both sides, then roll the salmon in the chopped herbs, being careful to coat both sides thoroughly.

3 Heat the remaining teaspoon of olive oil in a heavy ovenproof frying pan over a medium-high heat. When the oil is hot, carefully place the salmon fillet in the pan. Sear it for 3–4 minutes on each side, flipping once.

4 Transfer the pan to the oven. Roast the salmon for about 5 minutes until it is just cooked through. Cut the salmon into 4 portions and serve at once.

tip *Salmon is a fatty dish that is not high in mercury, so make this one of your first choices when you are opting for a fish dish.*

italian-style cod

rich in: ✓vitamin D ✓protein ✓omega-3 fatty acids

During pregnancy, try to restrict your seafood intake to 350g (12oz) per week. Eat a variety of fish, avoiding those known to be high in mercury (see page 35), which in large amounts can harm the developing baby's nervous system. Cod is a low-mercury fish, and this recipe is quick and simple, an ideal alternative to the typical battered deep-fried cod.

Preparation 10 minutes
Cooking 15 minutes
Makes 4 servings

250ml (8fl oz) milk

675g (1½lb) skinless cod fillet, cut into 4 portions

175g (6oz) panko (Japanese breadcrumbs) or other coarse dry breadcrumbs

1 tbsp dried basil

1½ tsp sea salt

100g (3½oz) pecorino cheese, finely grated

freshly ground black pepper to taste

2 tbsp olive oil

½ lemon, sliced into 4 rounds

1 Preheat the oven to 230°C/Gas 8. Pour the milk into a shallow bowl. Immerse the fish in the milk.

2 Combine the breadcrumbs, basil, salt, and cheese on a large plate. Season the mixture with black pepper. Remove the fish from the milk and coat it on both sides with the crumb mixture. Dip the fish into the milk again, then press into the crumbs for a second coating. Gently pat the fish to be sure the crumbs adhere.

3 Drizzle the olive oil on a baking tray. Place the fish on the tray. Bake for about 15 minutes until the topping is crisp and the flesh flakes easily. Remove the fish from the oven, garnish with the lemon slices, and serve at once.

RECIPE NOTES

• Other firm-fleshed white fish fillet, such as haddock and hake, can be substituted for the cod.

• Romaine Salad with Mint, Dates, Oranges, and Almonds (page 129) is an ideal accompaniment to this simple dish.

balsamic chicken with asparagus and parsley

rich in: ✓folate ✓iron

This folate and iron-rich combination will please your pregnant palate and help to expand your blood supply to support your growing baby. Chicken, like beef, is an excellent source of iron, and asparagus is a pregnancy superfood, rich in folate.

Preparation 10 minutes
Cooking 20–25 minutes
Makes 4 servings

4 medium skinless, boneless chicken breasts, about 550g (1¼lb) in total

1 tsp sea salt

1 tbsp canola (rapeseed) oil

5 tbsp balsamic vinegar

1 medium shallot, diced

350g (12oz) asparagus, cut into 5cm (2in) pieces

350ml (12fl oz) lightly salted chicken stock

25g (scant 1oz) fresh flat-leaf parsley, chopped

15g (½oz) unsalted butter

1 Sprinkle the chicken breasts on both sides with the salt. Heat the oil in a large frying pan over a high heat. Place the chicken breasts in the pan and sear for about 5 minutes until golden brown. Flip the breasts over and lightly brown the other side for 5 minutes or until the chicken is cooked through.

2 Reduce the heat to medium and pour in the vinegar. Cook the chicken, turning several times, for about 40 seconds until it has absorbed the vinegar. Transfer the chicken to a plate and set it aside.

3 Add the shallot to the pan and cook, stirring often, for about 30 seconds until soft. Add the asparagus and cook for 1 minute, stirring often. Raise the heat to high and add the chicken stock. Cook for 2 minutes. Stir in the parsley. Add the butter and simmer the sauce for a further 1 minute.

4 Return the chicken to the pan and heat through in the sauce for about 30 seconds. Divide the chicken among 4 plates. Spoon the sauce and asparagus over each serving and serve immediately.

RECIPE NOTE
• Accompany the chicken with Couscous with Olive Oil and Parsley (page 133).

chicken, sweetcorn, and black bean enchiladas

rich in: ✓fibre ✓folate

This simple meal uses three great convenience foods from your pregnancy storecupboard: canned black beans, readymade salsa, and frozen sweetcorn. Black beans are high in fibre, so try this dish in the third trimester, when you may need more fibre to keep things moving.

Preparation 30 minutes
Cooking 15 minutes
Makes 6 servings

4 tsp canola (rapeseed) oil

450g (1lb) skinless, boneless chicken breast, cut into 5cm (2in) pieces

5 tsp Mexican-style seasoning

1 tsp sea salt

2 garlic cloves, chopped

1 onion, diced

250g (9oz) frozen sweetcorn

1 can (about 425g) black beans, drained and rinsed

25g (scant 1oz) fresh coriander, chopped

12 corn tortillas, 15cm (6in) in diameter

350g (12oz) good-quality readymade salsa

175g (6oz) Cheddar cheese, grated

1 Preheat the oven to 190°C/Gas 5. Heat 2 teaspoons of the oil in a large saucepan over a medium-high heat. While the oil is heating, toss the pieces of chicken with 3 teaspoons of the Mexican seasoning and ½ teaspoon of the salt. Place the chicken in the pan and brown for 2–3 minutes. Turn the pieces and brown for another 2 minutes until cooked through. Transfer the chicken to a plate and set it aside.

2 Reduce the heat to low under the pan. Add the remaining 2 teaspoons of oil and then the garlic. Cook for 30 seconds. Add the onion and sprinkle it with the remaining salt. Cook for 3 minutes, stirring often. Add the remaining 2 teaspoons of Mexican seasoning. Stir in the sweetcorn and cook for 1 minute, then add the black beans and coriander. Remove the pan from the heat. Coarsely chop the chicken and add it to the pan. Stir well to mix.

3 Fill each corn tortilla with the chicken and vegetable mixture and fold into thirds (don't worry if the tortillas crack). Place on a heavy baking tray, packing the tortillas close together to prevent them from unfolding. Spoon salsa over each tortilla and sprinkle with the cheese. Bake for about 15 minutes until the cheese has melted and the tortillas are soft. Serve hot.

RECIPE NOTE
• To prepare a vegetarian version, replace the chicken with 450g (1lb) extra-firm tofu that has been drained and pressed (see page 102), then cut into 2.5cm (1in) cubes. The seasoned tofu will take less time to brown (just 1–2 minutes).

spicy chicken breasts with an avocado and sweetcorn salsa

rich in: ✓ folate ✓ iron

In hot climates, it is believed that spicy foods cool you down, so try this spiced chicken to cool your pregnancy-generated heat. The salsa is not your usual tomato-based version – avocado gives it a creamy texture and the fresh raw sweetcorn a pleasant crispness.

Preparation 15 minutes
Cooking 5 minutes
Makes 4 servings

4 medium skinless, boneless chicken breasts, about 550g (1¼lb) in total

½ tsp sea salt

5 tsp Mexican-style seasoning

1 tbsp canola (rapeseed) oil

Salsa

½ red onion, finely chopped

kernels cut from 1 cob fresh sweetcorn

25g (scant 1oz) fresh coriander leaves, chopped

juice of 2 limes

½ tsp sea salt

1 ripe avocado, peeled, stoned, and diced

freshly ground black pepper to taste

1 To prepare the salsa, combine the red onion, sweetcorn kernels, coriander, lime juice, and salt in a medium bowl. Gently stir in the avocado. Season the salsa with black pepper. Cover and set it aside while you prepare the chicken.

2 Sprinkle each chicken breast on both sides with the salt and Mexican seasoning. Heat the oil in a large frying pan over a high heat. Carefully place the chicken in the pan and brown for about 5 minutes. Flip the pieces over and cook for another 5 minutes until browned on the other side and the chicken is cooked through.

3 Divide the chicken among 4 plates. Top each portion with the salsa and serve.

RECIPE NOTES

• If fresh sweetcorn is not in season, you can use frozen.

• The salsa can be prepared several hours in advance and left at room temperature. The acid from the limes will prevent the avocado from discolouring.

tip *Avocados are a good source of folate and of heart-healthy fats. Early in the first trimester, folate is important in preventing neural tube defects.*

steak with many mushrooms

rich in: ✓ iron ✓ protein

If you are craving red meat, it may be your body's signal that you need iron. This steak slathered with sautéed mushrooms is sure to make your mouth water. Accompany it with a vitamin C-rich fruit juice, which will enhance your body's absorption of the iron. Calcium (from milk and cheese) and caffeine (in coffee or fizzy drinks) impair iron absorption.

Preparation 10 minutes
Cooking 15 minutes
Makes 4 servings

550g (1¼lb) rump steak, trimmed of all visible fat

1 tsp sea salt

freshly ground black pepper to taste

1 tbsp olive oil

1 medium shallot, diced

115g (4oz) chestnut mushrooms, sliced

115g (4oz) white button mushrooms, sliced

115g (4oz) portobello or flat mushrooms, sliced

120ml (4fl oz) red wine

15g (½oz) unsalted butter

25g (scant 1oz) fresh flat-leaf parsley, chopped

1 Sprinkle the steak on both sides with half of the salt and some black pepper. Heat the olive oil in a heavy frying pan over a high heat. When the oil is hot, carefully place the steak in the pan and brown for about 4 minutes. Flip the steak and brown the other side for 4 minutes. Transfer the steak to a cutting board and leave it to rest for about 5 minutes.

2 Meanwhile, reduce the heat to low and add the shallot to the frying pan. Cook for 30 seconds, stirring often. Raise the heat to high, add all the mushrooms, and sprinkle with the remaining salt. Sauté the mushrooms, stirring often, for about 2 minutes until they soften. Add the wine and simmer for a further 2 minutes. Stir in the butter. Reduce the heat to low.

3 Slice the steak thinly across the grain. Stir the steak into the sauce. Add the parsley. Divide the steak and sauce among 4 plates and serve at once.

RECIPE NOTES
- Sirloin steak can be substituted for the rump steak.
- Serve the steak with Mashed Potatoes with Olive Oil and Fried Garlic (page 134).

simply quick pan-fried steak

rich in: ✓ **iron**

Your blood volume expands almost 50 per cent in pregnancy, an increase that requires extra iron in your diet. Red meat such as beef is rich in haem iron, which is a form of iron that is well absorbed. Rump steak pan-fried with garlic and red wine has lots of flavour. The cooking times given here are approximate for medium cooked steak.

Preparation 5 minutes
Cooking 15 minutes
Makes 4 servings

675g (1½lb) rump steak, trimmed of all visible fat

1 tsp sea salt

freshly ground black pepper to taste

1 tbsp olive oil

2 garlic cloves, thinly sliced

5 tbsp red wine

120ml (4fl oz) lightly salted chicken stock

15g (½oz) unsalted butter

2 tbsp chopped fresh flat-leaf parsley

1 Sprinkle the steak on both sides with the salt and some black pepper. Heat the olive oil in a heavy frying pan (cast iron works well) over a high heat. When the oil is hot, place the steak in the pan and brown for 4 minutes. Flip the steak over and brown the other side for 4 minutes. Transfer the steak to a plate and leave it to rest for 5 minutes.

2 Meanwhile, pour off all but 2 teaspoons of the fat from the pan. Reduce the heat to low and add the garlic to the pan. Cook for 1 minute until it is soft and fragrant. Raise the heat to high and add the wine. Simmer for 1 minute. Add the chicken stock and simmer for another minute. Add the juices from the plate the steak is resting on. Stir in the butter and simmer the sauce for 2 minutes. Stir in the parsley. Remove the pan from the heat.

3 To serve, slice the steak thinly across the grain. Divide the slices among 4 plates and spoon over the sauce.

RECIPE NOTE

• When cooking steak, it is fine to have a bit of pink in the centre (medium to medium well-done), but during pregnancy you should not eat rare beef due to the risk of toxoplasmosis.

spice-rubbed pork fillet

rich in: ✓ iron ✓ protein

Pork has long suffered from a bad reputation for being fatty. However, the pork that is available today is very lean and tender, and a good source of iron. Pork cooks quickly, and serving it with a ready-made barbecue sauce makes this dish convenient and quick. Accompany it with mashed potatoes and coleslaw or a salad.

Preparation 5 minutes
Cooking 30 minutes
Makes 4 servings

2 medium pork fillets (tenderloins), about 550g (1¼lb) in total

1 tsp sea salt

1 tbsp Mexican-style seasoning

350ml (12fl oz) readymade barbecue sauce

1 Preheat the oven to 200°C/Gas 6. Sprinkle the pork fillets on all sides with the salt and then with the Mexican seasoning. Place the pork on an oven rack with a baking tray directly below it. Roast the pork for about 20 minutes until cooked through.
2 Transfer the pork to a carving board, cover it with foil, and leave it to rest for about 10 minutes. Meanwhile, warm the barbecue sauce.
3 Slice the pork and divide it among 4 plates. Top each portion with barbecue sauce and serve at once.

tip *Your baby gets the majority of iron from you during the third trimester, drawing it from you even if your stores aren't adequate. So you need to eat plenty of iron-rich foods.*

salty tuscan pork chops with caramelized apples and shallots

rich in: ✓iron ✓protein

These quick and delicious pork chops will appeal to your pregnant palate and fill your craving for salty and savoury foods in a healthy way. The sweet apples are a perfect contrast to the pork. Your whole family will be sure to enjoy this dish too.

Preparation 15 minutes
Cooking 30 minutes
Makes 4 servings

8 boneless pork loin chops cut 1.5cm (⅔in) thick, about 675g (1½lb) in total

1 tsp sea salt

freshly ground black pepper to taste

4 tsp canola (rapeseed) oil

2 shallots, finely chopped

5 tbsp red wine

120ml (4fl oz) lightly salted chicken stock

15g (½oz) unsalted butter

Caramelized apples

small knob of butter

2 Granny Smith apples, cored and cut into 1cm (½in) thick wedges

1 tbsp caster sugar

1 To prepare the apples, melt the butter in a large frying pan over a medium heat. When the butter stops sizzling, add the apple wedges, spreading them in a single layer. Reduce the heat to medium-low and cook the apples, stirring occasionally, for 10–12 minutes until they are golden brown all over. Sprinkle them with the sugar and cook for a further 3 minutes, stirring twice. Transfer the apples to a plate and set aside while you prepare the pork.

2 Sprinkle the chops on both sides with the salt and some black pepper. Heat 2 teaspoons of the oil in a large frying pan over a high heat. Add half of the pork chops and brown for 2½ minutes without moving them. Then flip them over and brown for about 2 minutes on the other side. Transfer the chops to a plate and keep warm. Repeat this procedure with the remaining oil and pork chops.

3 Reduce the heat to low and add the shallots to the pan. Cook for 30 seconds, stirring constantly. Raise the heat to high and add the wine. Simmer for 1 minute. Add the chicken stock and simmer for another minute. Add the juices from the plate the chops are resting on. Stir in the butter and simmer the sauce for 2 minutes. Remove the pan from the heat.

4 Divide the chops among 4 large plates and top with the caramelized apples. Spoon some sauce onto each plate and serve at once.

RECIPE NOTE
• The caramelized apples can be prepared several hours in advance, which will make this a really quick meal.

curried chick peas and tofu

rich in: ✓ fibre ✓ folate

Here's a zesty dish that will appeal to your altered pregnant palate in the second and third trimester. Both the tofu and the chick peas are wonderful sources of fibre, which will keep your bowels moving. The dish reheats beautifully, so it makes a great leftover lunch or simple supper during a busy week.

Preparation 30 minutes
Cooking 15 minutes
Makes 4 servings

Tofu

450g (1lb) extra-firm tofu

1 tbsp canola (rapeseed) oil

½ tsp sea salt

freshly ground black pepper to taste

1½ tsp curry powder

Chick peas

1 tbsp canola (rapeseed) oil

3 garlic cloves, thinly sliced

2.5cm (1in) piece fresh ginger, peeled and finely chopped

1 onion, thinly sliced

¼ tsp sea salt

1 tbsp curry powder

1 can (about 400g) chopped tomatoes, drained

1 can (about 425g) chick peas, drained and rinsed

25g (scant 1oz) fresh flat-leaf parsley, chopped

1 First press the tofu to remove excess moisture (see page 102), then cube it. Heat the oil in a sauté pan over a high heat. Sprinkle the tofu with the salt and black pepper. When the oil is hot, add the tofu to the pan. Sear it, without moving, for 1½ minutes. Stir, then sear for another 1½ minutes. Reduce the heat to low and sprinkle the tofu with the curry powder. Cook for 30 seconds. Transfer to a plate.
2 To prepare the chick peas, add the oil to the pan. When the oil is hot, add the garlic and ginger, and cook over a medium heat for 1 minute. Add the onion and sprinkle it with the salt. Cook, stirring occasionally, for about 3 minutes until soft.
3 Stir in the curry powder and cook for 30 seconds. Raise the heat to high, add 250ml (8fl oz) water, and simmer for 1 minute. Stir in the chopped tomatoes and chick peas. Bring the sauce to the boil. Reduce the heat and simmer for 5 minutes.
4 To serve, divide the curried chick peas among 4 shallow bowls. Garnish each portion with an equal amount of tofu and a sprinkling of parsley.

braised spicy black beans and brown rice

rich in: ✓fibre ✓folate

This combination of beans and rice is a perfect dish for the second or third trimester of your pregnancy, because it is light and not too filling, and will keep you regular. Eating spicy foods during pregnancy may help your baby acquire an early taste for new flavours.

Bean soaking overnight
Preparation 20 minutes
Cooking 2¼ hours
Makes 4 servings plus leftovers

300g (10oz) long-grain brown rice

50g (1¾oz) fresh flat-leaf parsley, chopped

60g (2oz) Cheddar cheese, grated

4 tbsp soured cream

Spicy black beans

450g (1lb) dried black beans, soaked in cold water overnight, then drained

2 tbsp canola (rapeseed) oil

5 garlic cloves, thinly sliced

1 onion, diced

1 red pepper, cored and diced

1 green pepper, cored and diced

2 chipotle chillies (dried smoked jalapeños) or other dried chillies

1¼ tsp sea salt

1 tbsp mild chilli powder

1 tbsp ground cumin

1 Preheat the oven to 180°C/Gas 4. To prepare the beans, put them in a saucepan, cover with water, and bring to the boil. Boil for 10 minutes, then drain.

2 While the beans are boiling, heat the oil in a large flameproof casserole over a medium heat. Add the garlic and cook for 30 seconds. Add the onion and cook, stirring often, for about 2 minutes until it is soft. Add the peppers and chillies. Sprinkle the ingredients with the salt and cook for 2 minutes, stirring occasionally. Add the chilli powder and cumin, and stir in. Cover the casserole and sweat the vegetables for 4 minutes, stirring occasionally.

3 Raise the heat to high and stir in the beans. Pour in 2.5 litres (4½ pints) water, cover the casserole, and bring to the boil. Transfer the casserole to the oven. Braise the beans for about 2 hours until they are very tender.

4 While the beans are cooking, prepare the rice. Bring 1 litre (1¾ pints) water to the boil in a medium saucepan. Stir in the rice and cover the pan tightly. Reduce the heat to low and simmer the rice for about 45 minutes until tender and all of the water has been absorbed.

5 When the beans are tender, remove and discard the chillies. To serve, place a scoop of rice on each plate and top it with a good scoop of spicy beans. Garnish each portion with a sprinkling of parsley, cheese, and soured cream.

RECIPE NOTE
• Leftover beans can be rolled into flour tortillas to make burritos or used to top warm corn tortillas.

crisp haddock with sautéed spinach

rich in: ✓ folate ✓ protein

There's that fried food craving again – this time for fish and chips! Rather than going to your favourite chip shop this weekend, make your own crisp-coated fish and serve it with folate-rich spinach instead of the chips. You need extra folate throughout pregnancy to increase your red blood cells and help with cell replication.

Preparation 10 minutes
Cooking 20 minutes
Makes 4 servings

60g (2oz) plain flour
½ tsp garlic granules
½ tsp onion salt
1 tsp paprika
½ tsp freshly ground black pepper
750g (1lb 10oz) skinless haddock fillet, cut into 4 portions
2 tbsp olive oil

Sautéed spinach

1 tbsp olive oil
1 garlic clove, thinly sliced
350g (12oz) spinach, chopped
juice of ½ lemon
good pinch of sea salt

1 Preheat the oven to 220°C/Gas 7. Whisk together the flour, garlic granules, onion salt, paprika, and black pepper in a shallow bowl. Dredge the fish in the flour mixture, patting it on gently. Shake the fish to remove the excess flour.

2 Heat the olive oil in an ovenproof frying pan over a medium-high heat. When the oil is hot, add the fish. Cook it for about 2½ minutes until a golden crust forms. Flip the fish over and transfer the pan to the oven. Cook for about 5 minutes until the fish flakes easily when tested with a fork.

3 Meanwhile, prepare the spinach. Heat the olive oil in another frying pan over a medium heat. Add the garlic and cook for 45 seconds, stirring often. Raise the heat to high and add the spinach, lemon juice, and salt. Cook the spinach, stirring constantly, for about 2 minutes until it is wilted.

4 To serve, divide the spinach among 4 plates, spreading it to create a bed. Place a portion of fish on each bed of spinach and serve at once.

RECIPE NOTES

• Plaice, lemon sole, and cod can be substituted for the haddock – all are low-mercury fish (see page 35). It will be necessary to adjust the cooking times accordingly. Thinner-fleshed fish may not need to be finished in the oven: they can be flipped and finished on the hob.

• A large (30cm/12in) cast-iron frying pan is the best pan to use for the fish.

oven-fried chicken wings

rich in: ✓ protein

Try this oven-fried version of a traditionally deep-fried take-away snack. It's just as tasty, but much healthier. Invite your friends over and enjoy these while you watch the big match or a movie on a widescreen TV. Accompany the wings with potato salad and a tossed green salad, and be sure to provide plenty of paper napkins.

Preparation 40 minutes
Soaking 1 hour
Cooking 20–30 minutes
Makes 4 servings

300ml (10fl oz) buttermilk

1.1kg (2½lb) chicken wings, tips removed and wings jointed

140g (5oz) plain flour

1 tbsp paprika

1 tsp onion salt

1 tsp garlic granules

1 tsp freshly ground black pepper

2 tsp canola (rapeseed) oil

1 Pour the buttermilk into a large bowl. Immerse the chicken wings in the buttermilk and leave to soak for 1 hour. Meanwhile, whisk together the flour, paprika, onion salt, garlic granules, and black pepper in a shallow bowl.

2 Preheat the oven to 220°C/Gas 7. Lightly grease 2 baking trays with the oil.

3 Drain the chicken. Dredge each wing in the spiced flour, shake off the excess, and place on the prepared baking trays. Arrange the wings 5cm (2in) apart. Place the trays in the oven and bake for 25–30 minutes until the chicken is deep golden and crisp. Serve hot or at room temperature.

RECIPE NOTE
• If your oven does not cook evenly, it may be necessary to rotate the baking trays.

tip *These zesty wings have all the fried flavour and texture of the fast food favourite, without the saturated fat and calories.*

chicken thighs with vinegar and sweet peppers

rich in: ✓iron ✓folate

Many think of beef as rich in iron, but you may be surprised to know that chicken is also a great source of well-absorbed iron. Both tomatoes and peppers help with the iron absorption. The sauce tastes very rich, because it becomes concentrated as it is cooked down.

Preparation 15 minutes
Cooking about 1 hour
Makes 4 servings

675g (1½lb) skinless, boneless chicken thighs

1½ tsp sea salt

2 tbsp olive oil

4 tbsp balsamic vinegar

3 garlic cloves, sliced

1 onion, diced

2 red peppers, cored and cut into 4cm (1½in) strips

350ml (12fl oz) lightly salted chicken stock

2 cans (about 400g each) whole plum tomatoes, drained and puréed

25g (scant 1oz) fresh flat-leaf parsley leaves

freshly ground black pepper to taste

1 Sprinkle the chicken thighs on both sides with 1 teaspoon of the salt. Heat 1 tablespoon of the olive oil in a large flameproof casserole over a high heat. Add the chicken thighs and brown, without moving, for about 3 minutes. Flip them over and brown for another 3 minutes. Drizzle them with 3 tablespoons of the vinegar. Reduce the heat to medium and cook for a further 1 minute, stirring often. Transfer the thighs to a plate and set aside.

2 Wipe the pot clean, then set it over a low heat. Add the remaining tablespoon of olive oil, then add the garlic and cook for 1 minute, stirring often. Raise the heat slightly and add the onion. Sprinkle it with the remaining salt and cook the onion, stirring often, for about 2 minutes until soft. Add the peppers and cook for a further 2 minutes, stirring occasionally.

3 Return the chicken and its juices to the pot and stir to mix. Cover and cook for 3 minutes, stirring occasionally. Raise the heat to high and add the chicken stock, puréed tomatoes, and remaining tablespoon of vinegar. Bring to the boil. Reduce the heat and simmer, uncovered, for 30–45 minutes, stirring occasionally. Stir in the parsley and season with black pepper. Divide among 4 plates and serve at once.

RECIPE NOTES
• Accompany the chicken with egg noodles.
• The dish can be prepared up to 2 days in advance and kept in the refrigerator. Any leftovers can be refrigerated, then microwaved for a delicious lunch at work.
• If more convenient, simmer the chicken, uncovered, in a 150°C/Gas 3 oven.

garlicky chicken and prawns with tomatoes and herbs

rich in: ✓ protein ✓ iron

It is generally no problem to meet your protein requirement in pregnancy. A good rule of thumb is to be sure you have a protein source at each meal. Chicken and prawns are both lean sources of protein. This dish is quick and simple, with lots of flavour for little fuss.

Preparation 15 minutes
Cooking 10 minutes
Makes 4 servings

450g (1lb) skinless, boneless chicken breast, cut into strips

1 tsp sea salt

4 tsp olive oil

2 garlic cloves, thinly sliced

250ml (8fl oz) lightly salted chicken stock

4 canned plum tomatoes, drained and diced

225g (8oz) raw king or tiger prawns without heads, peeled

15g (½oz) unsalted butter

4 spring onions, thinly sliced

25g (scant 1oz) fresh coriander, chopped

freshly ground black pepper to taste

1 Sprinkle the chicken strips with half of the salt. Heat 2 teaspoons of the olive oil in a large saucepan over a high heat. Add the chicken and sear for about 3 minutes until golden brown all over. Transfer the chicken to a plate and set aside.

2 Reduce the heat to low and add the remaining 2 teaspoons of olive oil to the pan. Add the garlic and cook, stirring occasionally, for about 45 seconds until it is soft and fragrant. Raise the heat to high and add the chicken stock. Simmer for 2 minutes. Add the diced tomatoes. Return the chicken to the pan and stir well, then simmer for a further 1 minute. Stir in the prawns and butter. Simmer, stirring occasionally, for about 1 minute until the prawns turn pink and are cooked through.

3 Remove the pan from the heat. Stir in the spring onions and coriander. Season with the remaining salt and some black pepper. Divide the chicken, prawns, and sauce among 4 shallow bowls and serve at once.

RECIPE NOTES
• Accompany the dish with couscous.
• Scallops can be substituted for the prawns. You will need to adjust the cooking times according to their size.

beef in red wine

rich in: ✓ iron ✓ vitamin C

Wine in cooking is safe in pregnancy, since the alcohol cooks off, leaving behind only the delicious taste. The intense flavours in this beef and red wine stew are sure to be transmitted through your amniotic fluid to your baby's growing tastebuds. Serve it with pasta or egg noodles sprinkled with a bit of grated Parmesan or pecorino cheese.

Preparation 15 minutes
Cooking 2½ hours
Makes 4 servings

1 tbsp olive oil

900g (2lb) boneless beef chuck or brisket, cut into 5cm (2in) cubes

1½ tsp sea salt

8 garlic cloves, peeled

1 onion, diced

1 tsp dried basil

½ tsp dried oregano

350ml (12fl oz) dry red wine

2 cans (about 400g each) whole plum tomatoes, chopped or puréed with juice

freshly ground black pepper to taste

1 Heat the olive oil in a large flameproof casserole over a high heat. Sprinkle the cubes of beef with 1 teaspoon of the salt. When the oil is hot, carefully add the beef to the pot and brown for 2 minutes without moving. Turn the beef and brown for another 2 minutes. Using tongs or a slotted spoon, transfer the beef to a plate.

2 Reduce the heat to low. If necessary, add a bit more olive oil to the pot, then toss in the garlic cloves. Cook them, stirring occasionally, for 1–2 minutes until softening. Raise the heat slightly and add the onion, basil, and oregano to the pot. Sprinkle the ingredients with the remaining salt. Cook, stirring occasionally, for about 2 minutes until the onion is soft.

3 Return the beef to the pot, along with any juices from the plate, and stir to mix. Cover the pot and cook for 5 minutes. Raise the heat to high and pour in the wine. Simmer, uncovered, for 2 minutes. Stir in the tomatoes and bring to the boil.

4 Reduce the heat and cover the pot again. Simmer the stew for 2 hours or until the meat is very tender, stirring occasionally. Skim the surface of the stew to remove any fat, then season with black pepper. Serve the stew immediately or allow it to cool and then refrigerate; reheat for serving (see below).

RECIPE NOTE

• The stew can be prepared ahead of time, and tastes even better when reheated, so make a double batch and reheat it during the week. It may be necessary to add a bit of water to thin the sauce.

desserts and smoothies

It is fine to have sweet things as part of a healthy pregnancy diet, so there's no need to deny yourself. Treat yourself to a small amount of your favourites from time to time – a piece of good chocolate, a small slice of rich cake, some home-made biscuits, or a scoop of ice cream. In general, if weight gain is a problem, it is not what you eat, but how much you eat. So exercise regularly, and eat slightly smaller quantities at your meals to allow room for a little dessert.

Cravings for chocolate and fresh fruit are two of the most common ones in pregnancy. Indulge them together, with some fresh strawberries or dried fruits such as apricots dipped in melted chocolate (to make your own see Chocolate-Dipped Strawberries, page 173). Try dark chocolate instead of milk chocolate, since dark chocolate is rich in antioxidants, which are heart-healthy and can prevent certain cancers. Some scientific data suggests that heart disease and cancer prevention can start as early as the diet your baby is exposed to in utero. Studies also suggest that mums who consume chocolate during pregnancy have babies with more smiling behaviour at 6 months of age. That will bring a smile to both of your faces.

Smoothies are a great treat, either as a snack, dessert, or even breakfast or a light lunch, since they are quick, easy, and delicious. For smooth sailing, keep a variety of frozen fruit in the freezer and stock up on vanilla yogurt. Yogurt is a great source of protein and calcium (300mg of calcium in 250ml/8fl oz). The RDA for calcium in pregnancy is 700mg, with the vast majority transmitted to the foetus to help form the skeleton in the third trimester. So pay particular attention to calcium in your diet after 28 weeks. If you are trying to gain weight, use a full-fat yogurt; to minimize weight gain, use a fat-free yogurt. Another protein food that can be substituted for yogurt in smoothies is silken tofu – use half of the amount given for yogurt.

mixed berry and yogurt parfait

rich in: ✓ antioxidants ✓ calcium

You eat first with your eyes, and these parfaits are as beautiful as they are healthy and delicious. Use pretty glasses and tower the fruit and yogurt high. All fruits contain a variety of nutrients, and there isn't one that gives you all that you need. So vary your fruits and you'll be more likely to get the array of nutrients that you and your baby require.

Preparation 10 minutes
Cooking none
Makes 4 servings

675g (1½lb) fat-free vanilla yogurt
150g (5½ oz) blackberries
350g (12oz) strawberries, sliced
150g (5½oz) blueberries
4 tbsp flaked almonds

1 Use a 175ml (6fl oz) dessert glass or wide wineglass for each parfait. Spoon a heaping tablespoon of vanilla yogurt into each glass. Add 3 or 4 blackberries. Add another heaped tablespoon of yogurt, then add 10–12 slices of strawberry. Add another heaped tablespoon of yogurt and then several (depending on their size) blueberries. Add a final heaping tablespoon of yogurt.
2 Garnish the parfaits with the flaked almonds. Serve at once.

RECIPE NOTES
• It is important to serve the parfaits immediately after they have been assembled. If they sit too long, they will become watery.
• Choose your favourite combination of berries or, if preferred, substitute small cubes of honeydew, Charentais or cantaloupe, or Galia melon. Melon is often well tolerated when you feel nauseous.

tip *You may find that in the first trimester, when nausea abounds, you can eat fruit but not vegetables. Eat a variety of fruit and you'll be fine. You can add vegetables later when you feel better.*

caramelized pineapple with honeyed yogurt sauce

rich in: ✓ vitamin C ✓ fibre

A perfectly ripe pineapple is arguably best simply peeled, cored, and sliced. But if you're craving sweets, enjoy it in this more decadent way. Cooking pineapple wedges in a small amount of butter caramelizes their natural sugars, making a uniquely sweet and delicious treat.

Preparation 10 minutes
Cooking 10 minutes
Makes 4 servings

15g (½oz) unsalted butter
1 pineapple, peeled, cored, and sliced lengthways into eighths

Sauce
350g (12oz) fat-free vanilla yogurt
3 tbsp clear honey

1 First make the sauce. In a medium bowl, whisk together the yogurt and honey. Cover the bowl and keep it in the refrigerator until serving time.
2 Melt the butter in a large non-stick frying pan over a medium heat. When the butter stops sizzling, carefully place the pineapple wedges in the pan. Cook them, turning 2 or 3 times, for about 8 minutes until they are golden and caramelized.
3 Transfer the pineapple to a plate. Raise the heat to high and add 120ml (4fl oz) water to the pan. Simmer, stirring to dissolve the caramelized particles, for about 1 minute until the liquid is reduced by half. Pour the liquid over the pineapple and serve, with the honeyed yogurt sauce.

RECIPE NOTES
• The sauce can be prepared up to 2 days in advance. Whisk it again before serving.
• If you prefer, serve the pineapple with vanilla frozen yogurt.

tip *While infant botulism, a very serious form of food poisoning, can be caused by feeding honey to children less than 1 year of age, eating honey poses no risk to you or your developing baby.*

chocolate-dipped strawberries

rich in: ✓antioxidants ✓vitamin C

Chocolate and fruit are delicious together and using dark chocolate adds a healthy dose of antioxidants. These dipped strawberries are also beautiful – they make a really special gift for Christmas or any other occasion. Just put a decorative paper doily on a tray and arrange the strawberries on top. They'll be eaten in a flash.

Preparation 20 minutes
Cooking 30 minutes
Makes 4 servings

1kg (2¼lb) strawberries
450g (1lb) good dark chocolate, chopped

1 Have ready 2 sheets of baking parchment. Rinse the strawberries well and thoroughly pat them dry with kitchen paper. Set them aside.
2 Place the chocolate in the top of a bain-marie pan. Pour water into the bottom of the bain-marie pan and bring to the boil. Remove from the heat. Place the pan containing the chocolate over the hot water (alternatively, use a heatproof bowl set over a pan of hot water). Melt the chocolate, stirring constantly.
3 Discard the hot water and refill the pan with cold water. Set the pan or bowl of chocolate over the cold water and stir until the chocolate cools a bit.
4 Working quickly and holding a strawberry by its green leaves with your fingertips, dip it into the chocolate, leaving a small portion uncovered. Let the excess chocolate drip back into the pan, then place the strawberry on the baking parchment. Repeat the procedure with the remaining berries and chocolate. Allow the berries to set for 15 minutes before removing them from the parchment.

RECIPE NOTES
• Choose the largest strawberries to dip.
• Be sure the berries are dry before dipping. Excess moisture will prevent the chocolate from hardening properly.
• Orange and grapefruit wedges, pineapple chunks, dried fruits, and large cashews or other large nuts can also be chocolate-dipped.

walnut and chocolate chip cookies

rich in: ✓ omega-3 fatty acids ✓ fibre

Imagine, a cookie that tastes good and that will help you have a smarter baby! These are made with walnuts and ground linseed (flax seed), so they are rich in omega-3 fatty acids, which help in your baby's brain and neural development. Linseed also adds a chewy texture and a dose of fibre. Enjoy these cookies throughout your pregnancy.

Preparation 10 minutes
Cooking 10 minutes
Makes 24 cookies

115g (4oz) unsalted butter
100g (3½ oz) caster sugar
115g (4oz) dark soft brown sugar
2 eggs
1 tsp pure vanilla extract
115g (4oz) linseed (flax seed), ground to a flour (see note)
210g (7½oz) plain flour
2 tsp bicarbonate of soda
good pinch of fine sea salt
175g (6oz) good dark chocolate chips
85g (3oz) walnuts, coarsely chopped

1 Preheat the oven to 180°C/Gas 4. In a large mixing bowl, cream together the butter, caster sugar, and brown sugar. Beat in the eggs and vanilla. Set the bowl aside for a moment.

2 In another bowl, whisk together the linseed, flour, bicarbonate of soda, and salt. Add this mixture of dry ingredients to the bowl containing the butter mixture and combine thoroughly. Stir in the chocolate chips and walnuts.

3 Place heaped teaspoonfuls of the dough about 5cm (2in) apart on 2 ungreased non-stick baking sheets. Bake for 7–9 minutes until golden and cooked through.

4 Remove from the oven and allow the cookies to cool and set for 5 minutes. Then with a slotted spatula, transfer the cookies to a wire rack to cool completely.

RECIPE NOTES
• The best way to grind linseed (flax seed) is in a clean coffee grinder. Alternatively, you can put the seeds in a deep bowl and grind with a hand-held blender. Cover the bowl with a tea towel to prevent the seeds from flying out.
• If you don't want to bake all of the cookies at one time, wrap the extra dough in cling film and freeze. Thaw the dough before shaping and baking.

smoothies

rich in: ✓protein ✓calcium

Early in pregnancy when you may be nauseous, soothing and mellow smoothies tend to be well tolerated, particularly when made with bananas and melon. They are deliciously sweet too. All of the smoothies here provide plenty of protein from the vanilla yogurt, so try a smoothie as a meal in the first trimester when nausea abounds.

Preparation 5 minutes
Cooking none
Makes 1 serving each

Orange creamsicle smoothie

100g (3½oz) orange sorbet

1 banana, peeled and sliced

175g (6oz) vanilla yogurt

250ml (8fl oz) orange juice

Honeydew and banana smoothie

350g (6oz) cubed honeydew melon

1 banana, peeled and sliced

175g (6oz) vanilla yogurt

250ml (8fl oz) apple juice

3 ice cubes

Berry pine smoothie

250g (9oz) pineapple chunks

125g (4½oz) frozen strawberries

250ml (8fl oz) pineapple juice

1 tbsp clear honey

175g (6oz) vanilla yogurt

For each smoothie, place the ingredients in a blender. Pulse 3 or 4 times, then blend until smooth. Pour the smoothie into a tall glass and serve immediately.

RECIPE NOTES

• For a lower calorie drink, use fat-free yogurt. For a higher calorie drink to help with weight gain, use whole-milk yogurt.

• Instead of yogurt, use 85g (3oz) silken tofu, which is a softer, creamier type of tofu that can also be used to make creamy salad dressings.

• For a different taste and texture in the Orange Creamsicle Smoothie, substitute 250g (9oz) cubed pineapple for the banana.

• In the Honeydew and Banana Smoothie, use Charentais or Galia melon instead of honeydew.

tip *Yogurt is an excellent source of calcium to build your baby's bones and teeth.*

catherine's peppermint bark

rich in: ✓ antioxidants

Chocolate is a delectable treat, whether you are pregnant or not. Share this delicious and incredibly easy recipe with your family. A culinary arts teacher in the United States developed it. Don't be intimidated by the idea of making sweets at home. This recipe is so simple that even children can make it!

Preparation 10 minutes
Cooking 10 minutes
Chilling 45 minutes
Makes 1.1kg (2½lb)

non-stick cooking spray

450g (1lb) white chocolate, broken into pieces

450g (1lb) good dark chocolate, broken into pieces

225g (8oz) peppermint candy canes or peppermint rock, finely chopped

1 Spray a 27 x 43cm (11 x 17in) baking sheet with non-stick cooking spray.

2 Place the white chocolate in the top of a bain-marie pan; put the dark chocolate in the top of a second bain-marie pan (or use heatproof bowls set over pans of hot water). Melt the two chocolates, then allow them to cool slightly.

3 Spread the melted dark chocolate as thinly as possible onto the prepared baking sheet. Spread the melted white chocolate over the dark. With a skewer or wooden cocktail stick, swirl the two chocolates together. Sprinkle the chopped peppermint candy canes over the chocolate.

4 Place a piece of baking parchment over the entire baking sheet and gently press the peppermints into the chocolate. Chill in the refrigerator for 45 minutes.

5 Peel off the baking parchment. Break the peppermint bark into pieces, working quickly so the heat from your hands does not melt the chocolate. Store the peppermint bark in an airtight container in the refrigerator.

nutrition charts

The following charts provide a quick reference guide to the foods you should eat to get the nutrients you need during pregnancy. On page 180 you will find a fruit and vegetable chart, and on pages 182–3 there are charts of useful information.

FOOD SOURCE	RICH SOURCE	SERVING SIZE	GOOD SOURCE	SERVING SIZE
FOLATE You need 400mcg of folate in your daily diet in the month before you become pregnant and in the first six weeks of pregnancy. Folic acid, a synthetic form of folate, is also acceptable. A rich source gives you more than 80mcg and a good source 40–80mcg.	beans, lentils, orange juice, breakfast cereal asparagus, spring greens or cabbage, kale, spinach, Swiss chard, strawberries, sunflower seeds	1½ cup-sized helpings ½ cup-sized helping	avocado, grapefruit, papaya broccoli, Brussels sprouts, cantaloupe, corn, peas, nuts, potatoes, salad greens, squash, raspberries, tomatoes, turnip greens, chicken, fish orange	½ fruit 115g (4oz) 1 fruit
CALCIUM Calcium builds your baby's bones and protects your own in pregnancy. You need 1,200mg of calcium in your diet every day. The rich sources listed here supply more than 150mg, and the good sources will supply you with 50–150mg.	ricotta cheese blue, Cheddar, Swiss or Romano cheese, sesame seeds tofu sardines (with bones) cabbage/spring greens ice cream, milk, orange juice, yogurt	¼ cup-sized helping 30g (1oz) 60g (2oz) 115g (4oz) ½ cup-sized helping 1 cup or cup-sized helping	almonds, Parmesan and mozzarella cheeses cream cheese, tempeh beans, broccoli, pak choy, cottage cheese, kale, turnip greens, yogurt (frozen) soya milk orange	30g (1oz) 60g (2oz) ½ cup-sized helping 1 cup-sized helping 1 fruit
IRON You need 30mg of iron in your body now to support the increased volume of blood in your system. The rich sources listed here supply 30mg, and the good sources will supply you with 1–2mg.	almonds, peas, sunflower seeds beef, dried peaches breakfast cereal (enriched) clams, kidney, haricot, or butter beans, lentils, pumpkin seeds, prune juice, soya beans, spinach	½ cup-sized helping 115g (4oz) 1 cup-sized helping	brazil nuts, cashews, dates chicken, pork, turkey, sardines, scallops asparagus, tomato juice egg	½ cup-sized helping 115g (4oz) 1 cup or cup-sized helping 1 large

FOOD SOURCE	RICH SOURCE	SERVING SIZE	GOOD SOURCE	SERVING SIZE
ZINC Zinc is an essential nutrient for growth and development in pregnancy. You need 50 percent more zinc in pregnancy and the recommended daily level is 15mg a day. Rich sources provide more than 4mg and good sources provide 1–4mg	peanut butter	1 tbsp	wheat germ	30g (1oz)
	beef, cheese, nuts, pumpkin	60g (2oz)	sunflower seeds	60g (2oz)
	seeds, chicken, chickpeas, pork, turkey	115g (4oz)	miso, raisins, prawns, tofu	85g (3oz)
	yogurt	175g (6oz)	potatoes, beans	115g (4oz)
	breakfast cereal, milk	1 cup-sized helping	orange	1 fruit
	oysters	6	lentils	½ cup-sized helping
	wholewheat bread	1 slice		
FIBRE Dietary fibre is important for good health at all times and is the best natural way to keep your bowels moving. Filling up on fibre can make you feel fuller for longer. A rich source offers more than 3g of fibre and a good source provides 1–3g.	avocado, apple, with peel, banana, carrot, nectarine, pear, potato (with its skin)	1 medium	cantaloupe, grapefruit	½ medium
	black beans, chickpeas, kidney beans, pinto beans (all cooked)	½ cup-sized helping	bran muffin, peach, pepper (red or green), potato (without skin), tomato	1 medium
	spinach (cooked)	¾ cup-sized helping	cherries	20
	celery (diced)	1 cup-sized helping	walnuts	10 halves
	cabbage/spring greens, peas **or** winter squash, Swiss chard (all cooked)	1 cup-sized helping	cashews	11 medium
			almonds	12 nuts
			peanuts	18 medium
	apple sauce (unsweetened), blueberries, grapes (with skins), strawberries, raspberries, watermelon, 1 slice 25cm (10in) in diameter	1 cup-sized helping	pine nuts	30g (1oz)
			sunflower seeds	2 tbsp
			peanut butter	1 tbsp
	rice, brown	1 cup-sized helping	tofu	85g (3oz)
			pineapple (diced), oatmeal (rolled oats), popcorn (popped), tomatoes (canned)	1 cup-sized helping
			romaine lettuce, chopped	2 cup-sized helpings
			wholewheat bread, granary loaf	1 slice

FOOD SOURCE	RICH SOURCE	SERVING SIZE	GOOD SOURCE	SERVING SIZE
PROTEIN Protein fuels physical growth and cellular development and most women have no problem meeting their protein requirements. You need 60g (2oz) of protein a day in pregnancy, which is about 3 servings. Vegetarians should aim for four. You need 3 servings of rich sources or 4–6 servings of good sources.	beans, cooked	1 cup-sized helping	milk	1 cup-sized helping
	cheese	85g (3oz)	peanut butter	2 tbsp
	eggs	2 large	sesame seeds	85g (3oz)
	lentils, nuts, sunflower seeds	85g (3oz)	tofu	115g (4oz)
	meat, poultry, fish	115g (4oz)	yogurt	1 cup-sized helping

FRUIT AND VEGETABLES	SOURCE	SERVING SIZE	SOURCE	SERVING SIZE
No single fruit or vegetable provides all the nutrients you and your baby need to be healthy, so you must eat a variety to obtain what you need. Aim for a minimum of five servings a day. Use this chart as a guide for serving sizes of the most common fruit and vegetable sources.	Fruit		Vegetables	
	apple	½ large or 1 small	raw or cooked vegetables	1 cup-sized helping
	apple sauce	1 cup-sized helping	lettuce	2 cup-sized helpings
	banana	1		
	grapefruit	1 medium	sweet potato	1
	grapes	1 cup-sized helping	beans (beans count as a protein and a vegetable)	1 cup-sized helping
	peach, nectarine, plum	1 large	tofu (tofu counts as a protein and a vegetable)	1 cup-sized helping
	pineapple chunks	1 cup-sized helping	tomato	1
	dried fruit, such as raisins, cranberries, cherries, dates, prunes	½ cup-sized helping	vegetable or tomato juice	1 cup-sized helping

FATS	FOOD	SERVING SIZE	HEALTHY FATS	UNHEALTHY FATS
You can have about three to four servings per day of healthy fats. Try not to have more than one serving from the unhealthy category.	avocado	½ fruit	high	low
	beef	115g (4oz)	low	high
	butter	1 tsp	low	high
	canola (rapeseed) oil	1 tbsp	high	low
	corn oil	1 tbsp	high	low
	Cheddar cheese	60g (2oz)	low	high
	margarine	1 tsp	low	high
	milk, whole	225ml (8floz)	low	high
	milk, 2% fat	225ml (8floz)	low	high
	nonfat milk, skimmed	225ml (8floz)	low	low
	nuts	85g (3oz)	high	low
	peanut butter	2 tbsp	high	low
	olives	10	high	low
	olive oil	1 tbsp	high	low
	safflower oil	1 tbsp	high	low
	salmon	115g (4oz)	high	low
	sunflower oil	1 tbsp	high	low

GOOD FATS	OILS	FOODS	BAD FATS	OILS	FOODS
Polyunsaturated fats Try to make up your fat supply by mainly choosing from this category or the one below.	corn, soya bean, safflower	fish coconuts and coconut milk	**Saturated fats** These fats can contribute to high cholesterol, heart disease, an increased risk of some cancers and obesity.	coconut	whole milk, butter, cheese, and ice cream red meat chocolate
Monounsaturated fats These fats are also categorized as "healthy", so choose from this range and the category above.	olive, canola (rapeseed), peanut	cashews, almonds, peanuts and most other nuts avocados, olives	**Trans fats** These fats are also unhealthy, so should be kept to a minimum.	partially hydrogenated vegetable oil	most margarines vegetable shortening deep-fried chips many fast foods most commercial baked goods

MILK COMPARISONS		FAT	CALCIUM	CALORIES	SERVING SIZE
Use this chart to see how much fat, calcium and calories are contained in the 4 main types of milk.	Whole milk	9g	290mg	150 kcal	1 cupful
	Reduced-fat milk (2%)	5g	298mg	140 kcal	1 cupful
	Low-fat milk (1%)	2g	300mg	120 kcal	1 cupful
	Nonfat milk (skimmed)	0g	301mg	90 kcal	1 cupful

PREGNANCY SUPERFOODS	FRESH ITEMS	REFRIGERATED ITEMS
These foods are supercharged with nutrients that are ideal for pregnancy. Favour recipes containing them.	asparagus blueberries cranberries salmon spinach	dark chocolate eggs enriched with omega-3 fatty acids yogurt silken tofu pasteurized cheese

PREGNANCY PANTRY	GROCERY ITEMS	REFRIGERATED/FROZEN	SNACKS	FRUIT/VEGETABLES
Keep a wide range of grocery items in your store cupboard and keep your refrigerator and freezer well stocked. This is especially vital in the third trimester and after your baby is born, when you may not be able to go shopping as often as before. Make sure you have the items on this chart on hand at all times.	anchovies (canned) chicken broth (low sodium) roasted peppers (jarred) salsa (jarred) tomatoes (tinned) sparkling water couscous pasta pearl barley rice (brown and white) oats wheat germ wholegrain cereals wholewheat bread baking powder baking soda brown sugar chilli powder cinnamon chocolate chips cumin Dijon mustard flour (wholewheat and white) honey sea salt maple syrup peppercorns (black) sugar vanilla black beans (tinned) cannellini beans and chickpeas (tinned) lentils navy, pinto, haricot beans (tinned) peanut butter canola (rapeseed) oil mayonnaise (low fat) olive oil vinegar (balsamic, cider) soya sauce (or tamari)	butter (unsalted) buttermilk Cheddar cheese cottage and cream cheese (low fat) eggs (omega-3-enriched) feta and goat cheese (pasteurized) Gruyère cheese half and half milk/cream mozzarella cheese (low fat) milk (whole and skim) Parmesan and Romano cheese sour cream (low fat) yogurt tortillas (corn and wholewheat) flax seed lemons lettuce (romaine and mesclun) orange juice (calcium fortified) turkey sausage tofu (silken and firm) blueberries chicken breasts corn green beans juice concentrate (apple, orange) peas spinach strawberries waffles (wholegrain) bagels (wholegrain) bread (wholegrain) muffins (wholegrain)	avocado broccoli florets with dip carrot sticks celery sticks cheeses (pasteurized) crackers dried fruit and nuts (mixture) granola hummus popcorn pretzels red pepper slices tomato and mozzarella (drizzled with olive oil) cashew nuts peanuts pecans walnuts pine nuts almonds dates prunes raisins apple rings (dried) apricots (dried) cherries (dried) cranberries (dried) sesame seeds sunflower seeds	apples bananas blackberries blueberries cherries clementines grapefruits grapes oranges plums peaches raspberries strawberries tangerines asparagus broccoli carrots cauliflower celery fresh coriander cucumber aubergines mushrooms parsley (flat leaf) red peppers tomatoes courgettes butternut squash ginger (fresh) garlic and onions potatoes shallots

first trimester one-week menu

In the month before you conceive and during the first trimester the high intake of folate in this diet will help prevent birth defects, such as spina bifida. You may also be coping with nausea now, and this diet will help you deal with symptoms.

	MONDAY	TUESDAY	WEDNESDAY	THURSDAY	FRIDAY	SATURDAY	SUNDAY
Breakfast	• 2 slices of wholewheat toast • 2 hard-boiled omega-3 enriched eggs (have two whites and one yolk)	• Wholegrain cereal • Melon slices	• Wholegrain toasted frozen waffles with sliced strawberries	• Honeydew-banana smoothie (p.176)	• Cantaloupe half-filled with calcium-fortified cottage cheese • Slice of wholewheat toast	• Toasted wholewheat bagel with cream cheese • Apple juice	• English muffin melt (p.100)
Lunch	• Vanilla yogurt, grapes, granola	• Wholegrain crackers, cheese chunks, and cantaloupe	• Avocado and cheese in a wholewheat wrap with lettuce and tomato	• Hummus on wholewheat roll-up	• Peanut butter on wholewheat crackers, grapes, skim milk	• Beef, barley, and escarole soup (p.125) • Crusty bread with olive oil	• Sesame tofu with orange-ginger broccoli (p.112)
Snack	• Toasted sweet potato-pecan bread (p.119)	• Frozen yogurt	• Dark chocolate-dried cherry scones (p.121)	• Watermelon	• Wholewheat pretzels	• Dried fruit and nut mix	• Flavoured rice cakes
Dinner	• Baked chicken breast • Baked potato with olive oil • Steamed spinach	• Baguette pizza (p.116)	• Couscous with spring vegetables	• Spaghetti with asparagus and toasted walnuts	• Spicy chicken breasts with an avocado-corn salsa (p.152) • Egg noodles tossed with olive oil, salt, and pepper **Or** • Baked potato with olive oil (if you are nauseous) • Vanilla yogurt • Honeydew melon slices	• Spice-rubbed pork tenderloin (p.156) • Mashed potatoes with olive oil and fried garlic (p.134) • Steamed asparagus **Or** • Honeydew-banana smoothie (p.176) (if you are nauseous) • Wholewheat toast	• Simply quick pan-fried steak (p.155) • Baked sweet potato • Steamed spinach **Or** • White rice with red sauce (if you are nauseous)
Dessert	• Orange segments	• Grapes and yogurt	• Apple	• Pear	• Papaya	• Peach	• Pineapple chunks

second trimester one-week menu

In the second trimester your appetite will return and many of the discomforts of the first trimester will ease, so you will enjoy your food again. You may find you are dealing with cravings. This diet helps you keep within the optimum weight gain.

	MONDAY	TUESDAY	WEDNESDAY	THURSDAY	FRIDAY	SATURDAY	SUNDAY
Breakfast	• Frozen wholegrain waffles topped with sliced strawberries and low-fat whipped cream	• English muffin melt (p.100) • Orange or apple juice	• Bountiful bagel sandwich (p.103)	• Nutty granola (p.104) stirred into vanilla yogurt, topped with sliced strawberries and a drizzle of maple syrup **Or** • Orange-creamsicle smoothie (p.176)	• Honeydew melon half-filled with calcium-fortified cottage cheese • Slice of wheat toast	• Hearty hot oats with dried fruit and nuts (p.95)	• Omelette with asparagus and Gruyère (p.92) • Slice of wholewheat toast
Lunch	• Cottage cheese, mixed fruit, wholewheat crackers	• Sliced turkey and Swiss cheese sandwich on wholewheat bread with lettuce and tomato • Apple	• Chilled pasta with broccoli, dried tomatoes, and spinach in a creamy dressing	• Wholewheat rollups with fresh mozzarella cheese, basil leaves, olive oil and salt	• Yogurt, granola and fruit	• Turkey sausage and broccoli rabe sandwiches (p.113)	• Stir-fried pak choy and sweet peppers with roasted tofu (p.108)
Snack	• Sunflower seeds with skimmed milk	• Skimmed milk poured over Nutty granola (p.104)	• Walnut-chocolate chip cookie (p.174) with skimmed milk	• Celery sticks with peanut butter	• Mixed nuts	• Melon slices	• Dried fruit and nut mix
Dinner	• Baked chicken breast • Baked sweet potato • Romaine salad with mint, dates, oranges, and almonds (p.129)	• Simply quick pan-fried steak (p.155) • Roasted asparagus with pine nuts and blue cheese (p.135) • Oven-baked potato wedges	• Herb and mustard-crusted salmon (p.147) **Or** • Braised kale with spicy sausage (p.136) • Couscous with olive oil and Italian parsley (p.133)	• Salty Tuscan pork chops with caramelized apples and shallots (p.157) • Mashed potatoes with olive oil and fried garlic (p.134)	• Broccoli and cheddar-stuffed potatoes (p.111) • Tossed green salad with olive oil and balsamic vinaigrette	• Chicken, corn and black bean enchiladas (p.151)	• Chicken thighs with vinegar and sweet peppers (p.164) • Couscous with olive oil and parsley
Dessert	• Stewed apple and yogurt	• Grapes and apple segments	• Peach	• Chocolate-dipped strawberries (p.173)	• Caramelized pineapple	• Blueberries with yogurt-honey sauce	• Mixed berry and yogurt parfait (p.171)

third trimester one-week menu

You may find you have an appetite now, but become uncomfortably full after eating very little. Eating small, frequent meals and the healthy, nutrient-dense snacks in this diet will ease you through the third trimester.

	MONDAY	TUESDAY	WEDNESDAY	THURSDAY	FRIDAY	SATURDAY	SUNDAY
Breakfast	• Canned unsweetened pineapple chunks with calcium-fortified cottage cheese • Wholewheat toast	• Banana	• Wholewheat bagel spread with light cream cheese and topped with sliced apples and raisins	• Sliced bananas topped with vanilla yogurt, drizzled with honey, and sprinkled with coarsely chopped walnuts and raisins	• Hearty hot oats with dried fruit and nuts (p.95)	• Eggs and Cheddar with salsa and corn tortillas (p.94)	• Swiss chard and feta frittata (p.117) • Wholewheat toast
Lunch	• Cheese chunks, crusty bread, and grapes • Frozen yogurt for dessert	• Yogurt with granola and fruit	• Hard-boiled egg salad (use 2 egg whites and one yolk from omega-3 enriched eggs) with low-fat mayonnaise and paprika, on wholewheat bread with Romaine lettuce and tomato	• Wholewheat rollups with tangy white beans and vegetables (p.114)	• Slice of vegetable or cheese pizza (treat yourself to a quick lunch out) • Green salad with vinaigrette dressing	• Sesame chicken salad (p.126) • Crusty bread	• Oven-fried chicken wings • Coleslaw
Snack	• Dried fruit	• Cheese on wholegrain crackers	• Dark chocolate-dried cherry scone (p.121)	• Carrot and celery sticks with divine dipping sauce (p.118)	• Sunflower seeds	• Raspberries	• Cranberries
Dinner	• Steak with many mushrooms (p.154) • Mashed potatoes with olive oil and fried garlic (p.134) • Cucumbers with onion, mint and feta (p.130)	• Garlicky chicken and shrimp with tomatoes and herbs (p.165) • Crusty bread with olive oil	• Beef in red wine (p.166) • Penne or other tubular pasta	• Seared salmon on wilted mesclun with raspberry vinaigrette (p.146) • Brown rice	• Balsamic chicken with asparagus and parsley (p.150) • Couscous	• Linguine with shrimp, tomatoes and parsley (p.145)	• Italian-style cod (p.148) • Romaine salad with dates, oranges and almonds (p.129) • Baked sweet potato wedges
Dessert	• Raspberries and yogurt	• Tangerine segments	• Plums and grapes	• Nectarines	• Sliced peaches drizzled with top-quality balsamic vinegar	• Apples sauce and yogurt	• Hot fudge sundae

postpartum recovery one-week menu

Just after you've given birth you are depleted emotionally and physically and your nutrient levels need replenishing as your body heals. This is not the time for a calorie-reduced diet. You need healing protein and energizing unrefined carbohydrates.

	MONDAY	TUESDAY	WEDNESDAY	THURSDAY	FRIDAY	SATURDAY	SUNDAY
Breakfast	• 2 hard-boiled omega-3 enriched eggs • Wholewheat toast • Orange juice	• Wholegrain cereal with dried fruit and skim milk	• Honeydew-banana smoothie (p.176)	• Nutty granola (p.104) stirred into vanilla yogurt, topped with sliced strawberries and a drizzle of maple syrup	• Cantaloupe half-filled with calcium-fortified cottage cheese • Slice of wholewheat toast	• Hearty hot oats with dried fruit and nuts (p.95)	• Breakfast burrito (p.102) • Orange juice
Lunch	• Sliced roast beef and provolone cheese sandwich on wholewheat toast with lettuce and tomato • Banana	• Spicy lentil and cauliflower soup (p.124) • Slice of crusty bread with olive oil	• Grilled cheese and tomato on wholewheat bread	• Spanish-style eggs with potatoes, onion and spicy sausage (p.93)	• Roasted provençal vegetables (p.139) topped with provolone cheese on a baguette	• Black bean and bulghur salad with parsley and lemon (p.127)	• Wholewheat bagel with cream cheese, dried cranberries, sliced almonds • Grapes
Snack	• Dried fruit	• Toasted Sweet potato-pecan bread (p.119)	• Sunflower seeds	• Celery sticks with cream cheese	• Spicy tamari almonds	• Baby carrot sticks dipped in hummus	• Flavoured rice cakes
Dinner	• Wholewheat rollups with tangy white beans and vegetables (p.114)	• Baguette pizza (p.116)	• Salad with lettuce, cheese chunks, cucumbers, avocado chunks, olives, and hard-cooked eggs with pumpkin seeds and balsamic vinaigrette • Crusty slice of wholewheat bread drizzled with olive oil	• Wholewheat pasta with sauce of olive oil, garlic and Italian parsley sprinkled with Parmesan cheese • Sautéed Swiss chard	• Swiss chard and feta frittata (p.117) • Crusty wholewheat bread drizzled with olive oil	• Seared salmon on wilted mesclun with raspberry vinaigrette (p.146) • Brown rice	• Broccoli and Cheddar-stuffed potatoes (p.111)
Dessert	• Blueberries	• Watermelon	• Nectarines	• Orange segments	• Banana and raisins	• Pear	• Mixed berries with non-fat vanilla yogurt

postpartum weight-loss menu

Once you have recovered and are ready to get exercising and get your body back, try this healthy diet to get the calories down, but the fibre and nutrients high. This will help you feel fuller sooner and help you lose weight in a gradual, healthy way.

	MONDAY	TUESDAY	WEDNESDAY	THURSDAY	FRIDAY	SATURDAY	SUNDAY
Breakfast	• Frozen wholegrain waffle topped with sliced strawberries • Vanilla yogurt, grapes, granola	• Wholegrain cereal with dried dates and skim milk	• Honeydew-banana smoothie (p.176)	• Nutty granola (p.104) stirred into vanilla yogurt, topped with sliced strawberries	• Cantaloupe half-filled with calcium-fortified cottage cheese • Slice of wholewheat toast	• Hearty hot oats (p.95) with dried fruit and nuts (eliminate nuts to lower the calories)	• One hard-boiled omega-3 enriched egg • Slice of wholewheat toast • Orange juice
Lunch	• Turkey and Swiss cheese sandwich on wholewheat toast with romaine lettuce and tomato with mustard	• Non-fat yogurt • Mixed berries, strawberries, raspberries, blueberries • 4 wholewheat crackers	• Hummus on wholewheat wrap with cucumbers, lettuce, tomato	• Wholewheat rollups with tangy white beans and vegetables (p.114)	• Cheese chunks, apple slices and wholewheat crackers	• Grilled cheese and tomato sandwich on wholewheat bread	• Salad of lettuce, cucumbers, feta cheese, red onion, and tomato with olive oil and balsamic vinaigrette dressing • Crusty bread
Snack	• Banana and yogurt	• Flavoured rice cake	• Cinnamon sugar toast	• Wholewheat pretzels	• Dates	• Baby carrot sticks dipped in hummus	• Air-popped popcorn and grapes
Dinner	• Romaine salad with mint, dates, oranges and almonds (p.129) • Baked chicken breast • Baked sweet potato	• Crisp haddock with sautéed spinach (p.162) • Half a baked potato	• Baguette pizza (p.116)	• Salty Tuscan pork chop with caramelized apples and shallots (p.157) • Oven-baked sweet-potato wedges	• Swiss chard and feta frittata (p.117) • Crusty wheat bread	• Steak with many mushrooms (4oz/115g) (p.154) • Oven fries (toss wedges of baking potatoes with olive oil and kosher salt and black pepper, bake in a single layer on a sheet pan at 425° F until golden, approximately 45 minutes)	• Broccoli and Cheddar-stuffed potatoes (p.111)
Dessert	• Pears and cheese	• Blueberries	• Pear	• Raspberries	• Grapes	• Banana	• Apple

index

Page numbers in **bold** indicate recipes and their illustrations.

tortillas 75, **94**, **102**, **114-15**, **151**
toxoplasmosis 35, 155
turkey sausage sandwiches **113**
twins 17, 38, 53

U
urine & urination 16, 31, 48, 51, 58, 62, 72, 73, 77, 82
uterus 16, 40, 48, 51, 58, 60, 68

V
vegans 32
vegetables *see* fruit & vegetables

vegetarians 19, 24, 25-6, 27, 28, 29, 112
vitamins 22, 28, 29, 30, 32, 63, 70, 82
    see also folate

W
walnuts 19, *27*, 63, **104**, **144**, **174-5**
water *see* hydration
weight
    obesity prevention 10, 13, 19, 27, 60, 70
    postpartum 80, 84
    underweight women 42-3, 47, 70
    weight gain 38-43, 46, 47, 60, 67, 68, 70, 106

see also birth weight; calorie intake
"white diet" 54, 57, 106, 143
wholewheat rollups **114-15**

Y
yogurt **29**, 101, 168, **170-1**, **172**, **176**

Z
zinc 30, 32, 179

Acknowledgments

Author's acknowledgments
I have been privileged to care for thousands of pregnant women during my years in obstetrical practice. The ideas and concepts in this book are dedicated to these women, their children, and their future grandchildren. It is our hope that this book captures both the art and science of eating, since food should be a pleasure, as well as the basis for good health.

Special thanks to Catherine Thomas, culinary arts inspector in the Cambridge, Massachusetts, Public Schools, for her recipe contribution of Catherine's peppermint bark.

Publisher's acknowledgments
Dorling Kindersley would like to thank the following for their contributions to this book:
Fiona Ford, nutrition consultant
Alyson Silverwood – proofreading
Susan Bosanko – indexing
Diana Vowles – editorial
Carole Ash – design development
Valerie Barrett – recipe testing

Annie Nichols and Valerie Berry – home economists
Tahira Herold – hair and makeup
Chloe Brown, Rachel Jukes and Isabel de Cordova – photography styling
Byll Pulman – photography assistance
Sarah Thorpe – design assistance
"Lovely-lovely" for supplying doilies
Modelling – Jennine Ellis, Liz Gough, Mala Mistry, Corrie Williamson, Agni Hardy and baby Leo, Marie Willsdon, Riyan Bissessar, Esme Folley, Yuko Tanaka-Betts

Picture credits
The publisher would like to thank the following for their kind permission to reproduce their photographs:

Alamy Images: Agencja Free 33, 36; Getty Images: The Image Bank 66; Mother & Baby Picture Library: 18

All other images © Dorling Kindersley
For further information see: www.dkimages.com